"Herrero—the H is silent and the R s rolled with a good Scotch burr."

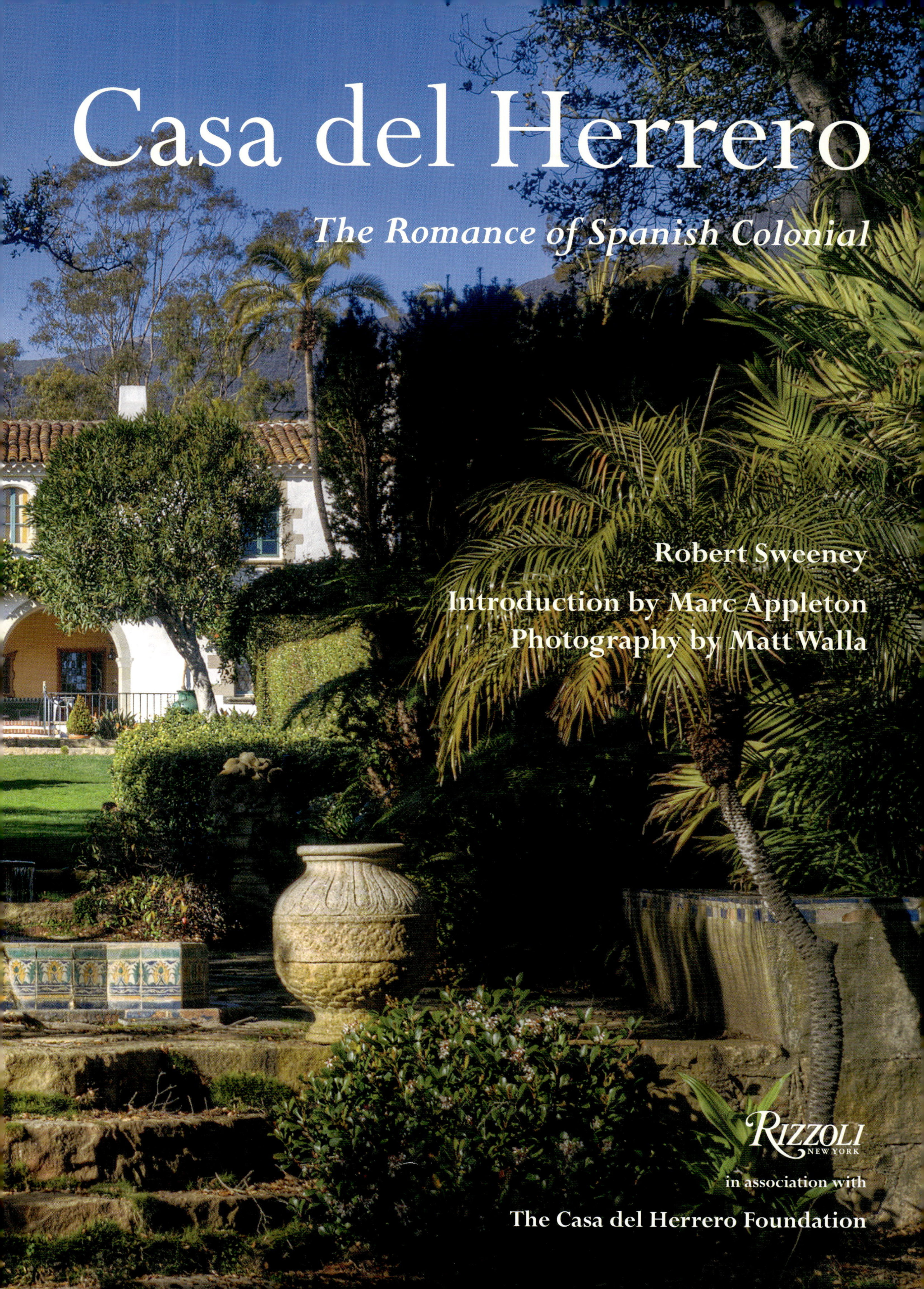

Casa del Herrero

The Romance of Spanish Colonial

Robert Sweeney

Introduction by Marc Appleton
Photography by Matt Walla

RIZZOLI
NEW YORK

in association with

The Casa del Herrero Foundation

First published in the United States in 2009 by
Rizzoli International Publications, Inc.
300 Park Avenue South
New York, NY 10010
www.rizzoliusa.com

2023 2024 2025 / 10 9 8 7 6 5 4 3 2

ISBN 13: 978-0-8478-3327-6

Library of Congress Control Number: 2009931110

Designed by Abigail Sturges

Printed in China

Page 1: Arthur Byne, pepper tree fountain.
Pages 2–3: South elevation.
Page 6: Entrance hall.

Illustration Credits

P. 19, Fig. 1.1: Environmental Design Library, University
of California, Berkeley
P. 20, Fig. 1.2: Environmental Design Library, University
of California, Berkeley
Pp. 24–25: Casa
P. 27, Fig. 2.1: Casa
P. 28, Fig. 2.2: Gerhard Sisters, St. Louis, Casa
P. 29, Fig. 2.3: Willard Thompson
P. 29, Fig. 2.4: F. D. Hampson Com'l Photo Co., April 1930,
St. Louis Public Library Archives
Pp. 30–31: Architecture and Design Collection, University
Art Museum, University of California, Santa Barbara
P. 33, Fig. 3.1: Casa
P. 33, Fig. 3.2: Casa
P. 34, Fig. 3.3: Casa
P. 35, Fig. 3.4: Casa
P. 35, Fig. 3.5: Collection of Patricia Gebhard
P. 36, Fig. 3.6: Louis La Beaume, Casa
P. 37, Fig. 3.7: George Steedman, Casa
P. 38, Fig. 3.9: Casa
P. 38, Fig. 3.10: Casa
P. 39, Fig. 3.11: Casa
P. 39, Fig. 3.12: Casa
P. 43, Fig. 3.14: Architecture and Design Collection, University
Art Museum, University of California, Santa Barbara
P. 48, Fig. 4.1: Pacific Coast Architect 24, no. 5 (May 1926): 11.
P. 48, Fig. 4.2: American Country Houses of Today (New York:
Architectural Book Publishing Company, 1927), 124.
P. 48, Fig. 4.3: American Country Houses of Today (New York:
Architectural Book Publishing Company, 1927), 124.
P. 51, Fig. 4.4: Smithsonian Institution, Archives of American
Gardens, Garden Club of America Collection
P. 52, Fig. 4.5: Casa
Pp. 52–53, Fig. 4.6: Lockwood de Forest Collection (1965-2), Envi-
ronmental Design Archives, University of California, Berkeley
P. 54, Fig. 4.7: Casa
P. 55, Fig. 4.8: Casa
P. 55, Fig. 4.9: Casa
P. 56, Fig. 4.10: Casa
P. 56, Fig. 4.11: Casa
P. 62, Fig. 4.18: Casa
P. 63, Fig. 4.19: Fred Dapprich, Casa
P. 63, Fig. 4.20: Lutah Maria Riggs, Collection of Patricia Gebhard
P. 73, Fig. 5.1: Casa
P. 74, Fig. 5.2: Montecito History Committee Archive
P. 75, Fig. 5.3: Fred Dapprich, Casa
P. 84, Fig. 5.23: Casa
P. 85, Fig. 5.24: Casa
P. 106, Fig. 6.2: Albert P. Hinckley, Jr.
P. 106, Fig. 6.3: Albert P. Hinckley, Jr.
P. 110, Fig. 6.8: Casa

To George Steedman Bass

Contents

Acknowledgments

I first visited Casa del Herrero in the 1980s. The undeniable beauty of the house and garden aside, my strongest recollection is the ease and graciousness with which Medora Steedman Bass allowed guests to wander through. By the time I returned two decades later the property had been opened to the public and it occurred to me that a book was needed but it took a chance encounter with Patricia Gebhard to provoke me into action. I am grateful to Pat for her initiative; this has been a rich and rewarding project. Pat read the manuscript several times and made valuable suggestions and, more importantly, she contacted Rizzoli on our behalf.

Diane Dodson Galt took the initial leap of faith in presenting this project to the Casa Board of Directors. I hope the results meet her expectations and I thank the board for its support and patience. There has been much friendly help along the way. Founding board members Dan Eidelson, Jean Smith Goodrich, Joan Jackson, and David Myrick all came forth with candid recollections. Over lunch, David emphasized the need to thank Dan Eidelson, especially, an easy assignment. Indeed I am particularly grateful to both David and Dan for their contributions to the Casa.

Albert P. Hinckley, Jr., and Margaret Hinckley Wise recalled visits to their grandparents' house over the years and contributed in other ways as well. Albert created the floor plans for this book. Margaret returned several pieces of her grandfather's silver to the Casa for photography.

Kellam de Forest graciously returned to the Casa to discuss his father's work there in the twenties and thirties and offered perspective that I otherwise would not have had. Jane Dyruff and I had numerous spirited conversations about the Casa and the Steedmans; Joyce Johnson filled in specific details. Barbie Henzell provided leads from her own research to various children, grandchildren and Steedman family friends. Alice van de Water gave me access to the archives of the Garden Club of Santa Barbara and Montecito. Edward Hartfeld, Edward Hart, Harold Acquistapace and Barbara Marra shared youthful experiences and photographs taken at the Casa. Daphne Ireland opened her house to Ed Hart and me and Jo and Willard Thompson provided sustenance on several occasions and shared their well-informed insights. All are thanked.

In St. Louis, Sheila Greenbaum and Gary Wasserman generously responded to my request to see their house at 34 Westmoreland Place, built by the Steedmans in 1909. Waller McGuire and Mary Frechette at the St. Louis Public Library provided invaluable information on the Steedman Architectural Collection and the staff of the Library & Research Center of the Missouri Historical Society was very helpful.

David Bisol of the Santa Barbara Historical Museum provided a collection of early photographs that reveal the Casa in various incarnations, often as work was underway. Michael Redmon and Kathi Brewster, Gledhill Library, Santa Barbara Historical Museum, and Kurt Helfrich, Architecture and Design Collection, University of California, Santa Barbara, responded to my frequent requests for information. Maria Herold, Curator, Montecito History Committee Archive, displayed at once her incomparable breadth of knowledge and contagious enthusiasm.

Donald Benson and Lynn Morris shared insights into restoration work that has been completed at the Casa. They also described numerous projects still to be undertaken.

Angelica Fuentes quickly obtained and translated obscure information from Madrid and Barcelona. Dr. James R. Marston was a thoughtful listener after hours and Nick Giudice provided shelter in Santa Barbara on numerous occasions.

The Casa staff has been unfailingly helpful. Jean Parry never missed a beat when she unearthed a new tidbit of information and Susannah Gordon and Olga Rogers stepped in to help with the tedium of last-minute details. José Aguilar and Sergio Martínez were always on hand at the right moment with good-natured responses.

Molly Barker inherited this project and shepherded the manuscript through various incarnations, intellectual, legal, and financial with tact and common sense. Randall H. Kennon, a friend—with his wife, Kathryn Smith—of many years' standing, helped with copyrights and permissions.

Marc Appleton, who wrote the foreword, has a rare appreciation of the Casa that can be traced back to his grandparents' own George Washington Smith house in Hope Ranch. He subsidized and arranged for Matt Walla to take all of the new photographs in this book. Matt's extraordinary images capture the Casa at its best.

A group of aerial shots—the brainchild of Albert Hinckley and one of which appears in this book—was brought to reality when Jo Duffy took Matt up in her plane. We thank Jo for her instantaneous support. We also thank Matt Efsic for technical assistance with the photograph of the entrance hall ceiling, as much a Chinese puzzle to photograph today as it was for Arthur Byne to assemble for Steedman in 1923.

Early on David Morton predicted, "This is going to be a fabulous book." He was right, of course, and he and his colleagues at Rizzoli, Abigail Sturges and Isabel Venero, have carried out the vision. All were delightful to work with.

Finally, I thank Mr. and Mrs. Ernest A. Bryant; Arthur and Barbara Henzell; Palmer and Joan Jackson; Charles T. and Anne G. Knight; Harry and Karen Kolb; Chapin and Cynthia Nolen; NS Ceramics; A. J. and Valerie Rice; and Mr. and Mrs. John H. Wise, Jr. Theirs has been an extraordinary display of support.

ROBERT SWEENEY
Pacific Palisades, California
April 25, 2009

Cutting garden.

9

Introduction

MARC APPLETON

In the history of residential architecture in California, there was perhaps no more impressively fertile period than the 1920s. During this decade, an eclectic regional architecture inspired by Europe but responsive to California's unique geography and climate was developed to a sophisticated level, and it was perhaps best memorialized by what became known as the Spanish Colonial or Mediterranean Revival. As the late historian David Gebhard observed, "In the twentieth-century American architectural scene, there has been only one brief period of time and only one restricted geographic area in which there existed anything approaching a unanimity of architectural form. This was the period, from approximately 1920 through the early 1930s, when the Spanish Colonial or the Mediterranean Revival was virtually the accepted norm in Southern California."

One of the greatest epicenters of this movement was Santa Barbara, and one of its greatest architects, George Washington Smith, practiced there from 1919 until his untimely death in 1930. Although he had majored in architecture in college, Smith chose a different career path, and it was only after some twenty years as a bond salesman and then an artist, that he was unexpectedly nudged into architectural practice after designing a house and painting studio in Santa Barbara for himself and his wife in 1918. As he later said, "I soon found that people were not really as eager to buy my paintings, which I was laboring over, as they were to have a whitewashed house like mine. So I put away my brushes and have not yet had a moment to take them up again."

Smith's design for his house was inspired by the Andalusian farmhouses he had seen during his travels through Spain, and its simple, spare yet picturesque architecture obviously appealed not only to him but a number of prospective clients. As R. W. Sexton later noted in his 1927 book *Spanish Influ-ence on American Architecture and Decoration*, "The peasant dwelling, or farmhouse of Spain, offers, perhaps, most for adaptation to American needs. Its chief characteristic lies in a pleasing combination of simplicity and dignity." Smith's subtle compositional artistry for his own house had struck a chord.

Among his earlier clients were George Steedman, a successful industrialist from St. Louis and his wife Carrie. After renting in the area, they purchased property in Montecito and hired Smith in 1922 to design a family retreat called Casa del Herrero (House of the Blacksmith). By 1922, Smith was already a respected architect, having embarked on or completed more than thirty projects in his first three years of practice, but this was to become one of the most demanding, protracted, frustrating, and, ultimately, rewarding of his commissions. It is fair to say that Casa del Herrero almost bookended his professional career. Although Steedman moved into the house in 1925, he continued to prevail upon Smith and his office in developing and tweaking its architecture and gardens. It was the most prolonged project of Smith's life, perhaps one of the most exhausting, but also one of his finest.

This book is not only the story of this spectacular place, beautifully captured in Matt Walla's photographs, that resulted from the journey begun by its client and architect—it also is the story of the journey itself. Robert Sweeney has given us a thoroughly informative and entertaining glimpse into the history, the intriguing characters and complicated process by which Casa del Herrero was created.

Most great houses and gardens result from a fruitful relationship among client, architect, and the other consultants and contractors involved. The business of planning, designing, and building a house is a complicated process, and behind many successful houses is often a complicated dialogue between the client and the architect. Such indeed was the case here. The design of the Casa proceeded from Smith's initial sketches in fits and starts, Steedman meticulously reviewing and fussing over the plans and, while initially praising the various proposals and schemes, subsequently questioning or rejecting particulars of the design as it developed.

Officially retired but still active and industrious, Steedman threw himself enthusiastically into the design process, educating himself as it went along. With the support of Arthur and Mildred Stapley Byne, the well-known antiquarians he hired to assist in sourcing and purchasing original artifacts, materials, fixtures, and furnishings from Spain for the new house, his design correspondence with Smith, while always characteristically diplomatic, assumed a more assertive and authoritative stance. The architect usually seemed to graciously accept his client's increasingly relentless thrust and parry in the struggle to resolve the plan once and for all, but there were moments when Steedman's endless changes strained the relationship.

When the plans finally came to rest long enough for construction to start, both the owner and architect seemed content with the overall result. In the last analysis, the design of Casa del Herrero is a combination of many influences, and it exhibits an intriguing duality—a sort of split architectural personality, which may owe something to this struggle. The northern front of the house, although embellished with some ornamentation, is distinctively asymmetrical, and its references to the simple, windowless Andalusian farmhouse precedents are still apparent. The southern garden facade, however, is more formal and symmetrical, presumably inspired by an Italian villa rather than a Spanish vernacular farmhouse. The gardens also exhibit both formal and informal influences, and they, too, were the product of extended discussions with several different landscape designers whom the Steedmans engaged over time.

It is interesting to note that both before and after Smith died, Steedman turned to other architects to remodel and add to his estate. With the exception of the jewel-like octagonal library by Smith's longtime assistant, Lutah Riggs, however, none of the other additions or outbuildings have any architectural merit comparable to the main house. The dynamic relationship between the two men and the architectural achievement they had accomplished together were not to be equaled again.

For all the attention it received during its design, the house remained surprisingly intimate in scale, and in this respect it successfully captures the spirit of the small peasant farmhouse that had been its original inspiration. In its details, however, it pretends towards something much grander and richer, and it is here that Steedman's personality is most apparent.

Detail of the shop.

There is little in the way of standard or carelessly conventional workmanship. Steedman was fastidiously attentive to all of the particular accommodations of historic architectural elements, tile designs and layouts, doors, fixtures, hardware and, last but not least, the artwork and furnishings. Although the spaces are intimate, in some cases even miniaturized, they are richly appointed and self-consciously detailed. Where the architect might have been content with a more modest but elegant simplicity, the owner seemed intrigued by including even more embellishments to enhance the romantic vision.

These elements and details were often ingeniously inventive, and perhaps more than any other aspect of the Casa, it is these touches which express the idiosyncratic character of the owner and make this house such a unique experience. A self-taught silversmith and metalworker, Steedman personally crafted many items, from furniture to light fixtures and hardware. Nowhere is his passionate obsession for invention more evident than in the workshop he built adjacent to the house. It is thoroughly and compulsively organized, every tool numbered and in its appointed place, with machinery powered by mechanical and electric devices that rival any of Rube Goldberg's fantastic contrivances. One has the sense that here in his shop, Mr. Steedman was blissfully in his element.

With most of the original furnishings intact, Casa del Herrero and its gardens were fortunately donated by the family in 1993 to a nonprofit foundation for the benefit of future generations. It is a remarkable gift, one that recently received National Historic Landmark status, the highest landmark award for historic places in America.

Like the house and garden, the idea for this book has also been a long time coming, nurtured and supported by many who have loved the Casa and cherished the unique place it holds in Southern California's history. Its publication is a welcome testament, not only to the enduring appeal of early twentieth-century Spanish Colonial architecture and gardens, but to the extraordinarily creative personalities that brought them to life.

*I am glad to tell you that your house in a general way is practically finished. I
 believe it is and will be considered the most successful house in the Montecito valley.
I mean this, and have never said it before about any other house. I feel certain that
you will be delighted with the result subject possibly to some minor details.*

George Washington Smith
to George Fox Steedman,
May 29, 1925

*Please do not consider these numerous changes in any way evidencing any
dissatisfaction with the house as it now is. We are thoroly [sic] pleased with it,
and it is only because we like it so much that we want to play some more with it.*

George Fox Steedman
to George Washington Smith,
September 28, 1925

*You remind me exactly of my father; he appreciates the simplified thing when it is
shown to him but by the time he has "perfected" it little remains of the simplicity.*

Arthur Byne
to George Fox Steedman,
March 24, 1930

CHAPTER 1

A Taste for Things Spanish

Spain seems like a room long locked, at the far end of a neglected wing in an old house. It is a room filled with strange treasures and the trappings of an historic past. Legends have grown up around these treasures and tales have been told that make the blood tingle and set the imagination on edge. Lands richer in art, such as Italy and France, have suffered by familiarity and their sweetness cloys a little from too much telling. They have been mapped and charted. Streams of tourists have made the beaten paths easy to follow, but Spain, geographically aloof, wrapt about in her ancient dignity and dreaming of her bygone grandeur, has made no sign of self-exploitation as the world marched on . . . .

Spanish scholarship has been negligent of its heritage and it has remained for two Americans, Arthur Byne and Mildred Stapley, to discover Spain for the Western world.[1]

Between approximately 1915 and 1930 an architectural style based on the imagery of old Spain took hold in the United States, principally in Florida and the Southwest. In some regions it came to symbolize a way of life. The most common and sanitized explanation for the groundswell of interest was a desire to revisit regional Hispanic roots. In fact, the new taste was fueled by contemporary scholarly inquiry and also by pilgrimages to Spain and Mexico in the late nineteenth and early twentieth centuries. And there were other, equally potent, catalysts at play. Intellectually, Spain was uncharted territory and, as such, offered the fascination of the new. Also, because of long-standing political and social strife and economic dislocation, it was ripe for plundering. Significant cultural artifacts could be acquired and sent home, an irresistible temptation to collectors.

The Hispanic Society of America, founded in New York in 1904 by Archer Milton Huntington, had a significant role in bringing awareness of Spain to the forefront in the early twentieth century. Huntington was the stepson of the railroad magnate Collis P. Huntington. As a young man with enormous financial resources, he assembled an unprecedented collection of paintings, decorative art, books, manuscripts, maps, prints, and photographs that became the underpinning of his museum. In 1904 he also acquired property in Audubon Park between 155th and 156th Streets and Broadway in Manhattan and commissioned his nephew, Charles P. Huntington, to design a building in the Beaux Arts style to house the society's activities. The Society opened to the public in 1908. Huntington's program was ambitious and included exhibitions and publications on virtually all aspects of Spanish culture, in addition to collecting.[2]

Huntington did not initially address architecture with its allied arts. The moving forces for this field of study were Arthur Byne, then a young architect working for Howells and Stokes in New York, and his wife Mildred Stapley. Byne (1884?–1935) enrolled in the Architecture Department at the University of Pennsylvania as a special student in 1903. He received a Certificate of Proficiency in Architecture in December 1905 and then spent a year at the American Academy in Rome.[3] Stapley (1875?–1941) left a less easily verifiable trail. She is identified in the 1910 census as a widowed magazine writer; her obituary mentions that she was a portrait painter who was ". . . so aroused by an El Greco portrait of a Spaniard that she resolved to study the Spanish masters in their own land." Both she and her future husband were predisposed to express themselves in print and published several early essays on topics well removed from the subsequent work that secured their reputations. Three articles by Stapley that appeared between 1906 and 1909 describe youthful experiences in Paris; though in the third person, one is tempted to interpret them as semi-autobiographical. Byne began in 1909 with an article on Williamsburg, long before the Rockefeller restoration.[4] After their marriage in 1910 the Bynes traveled through Spain, he sketching and taking photographs. They used a book published in 1865, *Some Account of Gothic Architecture in Spain* by George Street, a British architect, as their guide.[5]

The Bynes returned to New York from Spain in November 1910. In the following two years they recorded their impressions in a group of articles published in the *Architectural Record* and *American*

The
Architectural
Record
June
1917
JUN 22 1917
PUBLISHED IN NEW YORK
35 ¢ A Copy $ 3.00 A Year

The ARCHITECTVRAL RECORD

Architect, firmly establishing themselves among the earliest pamphleteers of the new interest in Spanish architecture. Stapley first wrote on iron grilles, or *rejas*, describing the difficulty of working with the "... inexpensive, dull-colored, stubborn ..." material and the refinement that could be achieved. She noted, "The simplest house has grilles at the ground floor at least, and at the upper windows iron railed balconies supported by brackets and scrolls of interesting design. It is surprising the degree to which a window grille excludes the sun, in addition to its first purpose of protecting and screening the inmates."[6]

Clearly anticipating the new Spanish taste in architecture, in 1911 Byne observed of Casa del Greco in Toledo: "It is not often that the simpler sort of American domestic work has a chance to benefit by the frequent house restoration going on abroad. ... But the recent rehabilitation of the house of El Greco ... presents a very thorough picture of a simple Spanish Sixteenth Century residence, and one that might readily be adapted for an American summer home to-day." Perhaps of more specific interest in a discussion of Casa del Herrero was Byne's description of the fireplace in the kitchen: "An enormous hood ... projects about four feet over the hearth ... and at right angles ... are brick seats forming a sort of inglenook arrangement."[7]

With an introduction from his affluent and socially prominent mentor I. N. Phelps Stokes, Byne approached Huntington in late 1913 about publishing a book on Spanish Renaissance architecture. He also mentioned the large group of photographs that he had taken in Spain. Byne's overture led to an association with the Hispanic Society that existed in various guises between 1914 and 1921. In that period the Society published four well-received studies of Spanish architecture by Byne and Stapley, underwrote a photographic expedition to Spain, and mounted an exhibition of their photographs. For two years, 1916–18, the Bynes served as curators of architecture and the allied arts.[8] At the same time they continued to publish articles with Spanish themes in various periodicals. Also, reproductions of Byne's watercolor drawings of Spanish buildings appeared on the covers of fifteen issues of *Architectural Record* between 1911 and 1920 (Figs. 1.1, 1.2). As propaganda the importance of these covers cannot be overestimated.[9]

The Bynes' first book published by the Hispanic Society, *Rejería of the Spanish Renaissance*, on church screens, appeared in 1914. Bertram Goodhue, in his review, commented on "This remarkably written, remarkably illustrated, and remarkably printed volume. ... All in all, among the unending flood of architectural books this stands out conspicuously as one of the very best ever issued in America. ..." Similarly, Marrion Wilcox, writing in *Architectural Record* praised *Spanish Ironwork*, published in 1915, as "... a very genuine and sufficiently extended treatise."[10]

Spanish Architecture of the Sixteenth Century followed in 1917. Clearly engaged by the Bynes' work, Wilcox observed "... as time passed the fact became evident that we stood in need of a good new book on the Plateresque, simply because so few critics, either Spanish or foreign, had ever 'ventured into the Renaissance century, the epoch of civil rather than ecclesiastical building activity.' It is a pleasure to say that such a book has finally been written and published in attractive form under the auspices of the Hispanic Society of America. ..." *Decorated Wooden Ceilings in Spain*, 1920, was the Bynes' final work for the Hispanic Society. Like the others, it was greeted with approbation. William Lawrence Bottomley, a school friend of Byne's whose own book, *Spanish Details*, was published in 1924, found it "thorough and scholarly ..." but "... to be chiefly commended for its illustrations. ... It is the physical appearance of the object of art that is of primary importance, and here the book excels."[11]

Clearly the Bynes positioned themselves to both create and fuel the new Spanish taste. They also established a network of connections that served them well. The Hispanic Society, however, interpreted their actions as self-serving. They were removed as curators at the end of 1918 and reengaged "on behalf of the society for the preparation of literary material in Spain."[12] Huntington followed up in January commenting that they did their work well but "they have limitations which may be hard to conquer. Vanity is their danger."[13] Mildred Stapley referred later to a "certain threat" (from Huntington) that they would be "chopped to mincemeat."[14] Still there seems never to have been a formal acrimonious break. Remnants of the association with the Society lingered until 1927, and the Bynes maintained contact until at least 1934.[15]

Spanish Colonial Revival architecture as it developed in the twentieth century was an admixture of Hispanic styles that owed as much to Mexico as to Spain. The 1915 Panama-California International Exposition in San Diego typically serves as the point of departure for discussion. The exposition was described at the time by its principal architect, Bertram Goodhue, as an homage to the Spanish *Conquistadores*—a nostalgic and romanticized vision

Fig. 1.2: Arthur Byne, Arco de la Sangre, Toledo.

of the Hispanic heritage—and justified later as confirming and consolidating the architectural traditions of the region.[16] Goodhue was among the earliest American architects to travel to Mexico and record his impressions. His first book, *Mexican Memories,* based on an 1891 trip, was published the following year. After a second trip in 1899 with Sylvester Baxter, a Boston journalist, he contributed plans to Baxter's book, *Spanish-Colonial Architecture in Mexico,* published in 1901.[17] Goodhue's biographer, Richard Oliver, concluded, " . . . Goodhue's designs prepared the way both for the more academic work of people like Myron Hunt and for the freer work of George Washington Smith. . . . "[18]

Palm Beach and Santa Barbara are the meccas of Spanish Colonial Revival architecture in the United States. Neither was designed as a Spanish city; in both cases Hispanic buildings replaced existing Victorian construction though with distinct regional variations. Henry Flagler developed Palm Beach as a winter resort for the very rich after he realized that St. Augustine, where he had built the Ponce de Leon and Alcazar Hotels between 1885 and 1888 in an attempt to create a "winter Newport," was in fact too cold. He extended his railroad, known as the "Flagler System," to West Palm Beach in 1894, the same year his first hotel in Palm Beach, the Royal Poinciana, opened. Two years later he built the Palm Beach Inn, which he renamed the Breakers in 1901.

More than any other architect, Addison Mizner was responsible for the prevailing architectural idiom in Palm Beach. As James Marston Fitch amusingly pointed out, Mizner's " . . . preparation . . . was . . . extracurricular in the most literal sense of the word. He finished no schools, gained no degrees, and only won a license to practice under the so-called 'grandfather clause' of registration at the age of forty-seven." Yet between 1918, when he first arrived in Florida, and 1925, Mizner ". . . transformed the shingle cottage, bungalow, and yellow hotel town of Henry M. Flagler into a resort of fashion and elegance in the 'Spanish style.'"[19]

Mizner, like George Washington Smith, had traveled in Spain but his interpretations of Spanish architecture tended to be compositionally restless and relied more on Baroque flourishes than the asceticism Smith favored. He also incorporated many Venetian Gothic details. The Everglades Club, designed and built in 1918–19, established him socially and architecturally in Palm Beach. In the next five years he built and furnished houses there for some of the richest members of American society and, in the process, incurred the scorn of Arthur Byne.

Santa Barbara's history can be traced to the establishment of a presidio in 1782 as a midpoint between San Francisco and San Diego, and a mission, founded in 1786. Santa Barbara was incorporated in 1850 and developed as a Victorian frontier town on a grid plan; real growth occurred after the arrival of the Southern Pacific Railroad 1887. Because of its climate and idyllic setting it became a destination for tourists early on. The Arlington Hotel opened in 1876, followed by the Potter in 1903.

Montecito immediately to the east took form very differently. Land was first allocated formally in the nineteenth century in a series of pueblo (Mexican) land grants that were cultivated as orchards and farms. Much of its layout today is a carryover from these agrarian roots. Streets were laid out randomly; Hot Springs Road originally was an Indian trail. The first zoning ordnance was enacted in 1929, and most of the area remains unincorporated today. Though earlier houses had been built, the transition from farmland to estates began in the 1890s.

By 1915 Montecito was well established as a colony for the affluent. A contemporary *Los Angeles Times* article describes:

> . . . scattered elegant homes, costing hundreds of thousands of dollars, the homes of people of wealth and refinement from all over the world . . . It is a rare combination of balmy airs and peerless landscapes. . . . Some of the homes, with their parklike surroundings, are "dreams" of beauty.[20]

Architecturally Santa Barbara and Montecito evolved from a vaguely defined Mediterranean aesthetic to a passion for architecture inspired by Andalusian prototypes. Two large houses in Montecito, one for Henry Dater (now Val Verde, designed by Goodhue in 1915) and the other for John P. Jefferson (now the Music Academy of the West, a 1916 remodeling by Reginald Johnson of a building originally designed by Francis Wilson), are the earliest and most prominent Mediterranean examples. They are defined by severe cubic masses and planar wall surfaces; the Jefferson house is embellished by *churrigueresque,* or Spanish Baroque, ornament around the entry. The Peshine house, now Shoreline Community Church, designed in 1917 by Myron Hunt, moves decisively toward a more specifically Spanish idiom with its *rejas,* or iron window grilles, and, especially, its Spanish Colonial chapel.[21]

Though based in Pasadena, Reginald Johnson designed several grand estates in Montecito. His aptitude for Spanish Colonial Revival design can be traced to his collaboration with Carleton M.

Winslow on a precocious 1914 chapel for the Harvard School for Boys in Los Angeles.[22] But he was not fully committed that early. His 1919 house for E. Palmer Gavit (now Lotusland) has Spanish overtones, but as a group his Montecito houses are sober asymmetrical exercises, neither Italian nor Spanish, whose commanding presence depends more on considerable size than stylistic reference. He justified his designs as regional responses in 1930:

> The future of architecture in California should be based first on conditions that exist. No architecture has ever been developed in any part of the world which has been contrary to the climate of the country. . . . When I first went to California, I wanted to take the various styles of the past, particularly of Spain and Italy, and to adapt them to a semi-tropical climate.
>
> . . . the house of Mr. J. P. Jefferson at Montecito . . . is the Spanish type. . . . Its design is modelled on Bertram Goodhue's architecture of the San Diego Exposition . . . —Bertram Goodhue whom we all revere.[23]

These statements notwithstanding, only in 1928 with his masterful design for the Santa Barbara Biltmore Hotel did Johnson fully embrace the Spanish style.

It fell to James Osborne Craig, a Scottish architect, and George Washington Smith to introduce the Andalusian vernacular so celebrated today in Santa Barbara. Craig left two buildings of such potency—even precocity, given his age—completed posthumously, that one suspects he would have given Smith ample competition if not for his premature death. His patron Bernhard Hoffmann, who went on to figure prominently in the rebuilding of Santa Barbara after the 1925 earthquake, commissioned both. One was Hoffmann's own house; the other was El Paseo, a complex of shops and an open-air restaurant arranged around existing nineteenth-century adobes. Each was selected for recognition in the "Better Architecture Competition" held in 1924; the house received honorable mention. El Paseo was identified as one of "the ten most notable examples of architecture in Santa Barbara and vicinity." The jury justified its decision:

> El Paseo is notable for the informal novelty and interest of its plan; the incident and charm of its various parts. These buildings as a group embody to an unusual degree the romance and quality of the architectural tradition associated with the early years of California, one well adapted to this arid climate with its bright sunshine and deep shadows. There is an inspiration here that should have great effect in the development of Californian architecture.[24]

George Washington Smith (1876–1930) began practicing architecture in 1918 after earlier careers as a bond salesman and painter. Although certainly his reputation rests on his Spanish Colonial Revival buildings, he worked in other styles as well as Patricia Gebhard details in her definitive book on the architect. His designs included forays into German and Italian vernacular; he also concocted a unique "Byzantine" house in Pebble Beach. Gebhard's research has established that he built his groundbreaking house on Middle Road in Montecito in 1918, two years later than previously thought. Even so, with the possible exception of a few less significant works by Craig for which dates have not been established, this is the first specifically Andalusian building in Santa Barbara. By 1922 when Steedman hired him, after a scant four years of practice and the untimely death of James Osborne Craig, Smith had established himself as the most important proponent of Spanish Colonial Revival architecture in Santa Barbara. In his office at the time were projects for City Hall Plaza and the new Lobero Theatre; designs for the Daily News building were under way a month later.[25]

CHAPTER 2

The Steedmans of St. Louis

George Fox Steedman (1871–1940) and his brothers Harrison (1867–1921) and Edwin (1873–1961) made their money at Curtis & Company, a St. Louis manufacturer of saws, sawmill and pneumatic machinery that was acquired by their father in the late nineteenth century. George joined the company in August 1893 and became president in 1904.[1] The windfall came during World War I when they produced munitions first for the British government, then the American (Fig. 2.1). George Steedman explained:

After the sinking of the *Lusitania* in 1915, I was convinced that it was only a question of time before the United States would be drawn into the War, so our company, of which I was then president, solicited an ammunition contract from the British Government, which was awarded us in October, 1915, for 8-inch high explosive projectile forgings. We designed and built for the British Government a plant with special equipment, and had it in quantity operation in less than three months' time. After we had been running a few months our contracts were doubled, and after a few additional months, redoubled.

When the United States went into the War in 1917, our work for the British Government was stopped, and after a very trying shut-down of several months, we were given still larger contracts by the American Government on which we worked until the end of the War.

Our total combined output for both governments was over two and a half million projectile forgings, ranging in size from 155 mm. to 240 mm. We made some very important process inventions which more than doubled the previous records of production, and which, although patented, we gave without charge to the Ordnance Department.[2]

George Steedman graduated from Harvard magna cum laude with an A.B. degree in 1892. His one surviving diary from the time suggests an articulate twenty-year-old financially comfortable but not rich, capable of introspection and with a capacity for intense intellectual application (he called it "grinding"). There also was a propensity for self-sufficiency. He noted at one point that he was ". . . dead broke [and] shall have to write home for money. . . . I hate to ask for money. I shall feel much more manly when I spend my own money." And there was a lighter side. Returning to Cambridge from Cincinnati on January first, 1891, he shared a drawing room on the train with two friends; they amused themselves playing poker. After losing $7.50 he observed, "Poker is lots of fun but expensive for a young fellow." Back in Cambridge he found "One very indignant letter. . . . Girls never know what they think."[3]

In 1903 Steedman and Carrie Robb Howard (1874–1962) were married at Christ Church Cathedral in St. Louis. The event was reported as ". . . one of the most brilliant nuptial affairs of the season . . . not only fashionable in point of principals and guests, but exceedingly well arranged and a beautiful spectacle."[4] Carrie Howard was an experienced and well-traveled young woman. She was an 1892 graduate of the Mary Institute, a girls' preparatory school founded in 1859 as an affiliate of Washington University, and subsequently attended boarding school in New York City.[5] She went to California in 1896, stopping in Coronado, Los Angeles, and Santa Barbara and, on the return trip, El Paso to attend to her family's real estate interests there.[6] Three trips to Europe—each of several months' duration—followed in 1897, 1899, and 1901.[7] Her parents' house at 33 Vandeventer Place, a post–Civil War enclave for the affluent in St. Louis, suggests

economic status superior to Steedman's; a 1913 newspaper article identifies her widowed mother as " . . . said to be the richest woman in St. Louis."[8] After their marriage the Steedmans settled in a modest house at 3944 Westminster Place, though they returned often to 33 Vandeventer and their two daughters were born there, Katherine in 1904 and Medora in 1909 (Fig. 2.2).

The Steedmans showed evidence of social ambition early on. Beginning in 1904 the St. Louis Social Register regularly listed their memberships in the Racquet, University, Noonday, and St. Louis Country Clubs, among others. And they did not remain long on Westminster. In 1905 they acquired property on Westmoreland Place, signaling their intention to build something more substantial.[9] Westmoreland and the adjoining Portland Places were established in 1888 as the Forest Park Addition which, like Vandeventer, was laid out by Julius Pritzman, a civil engineer and surveyor of German descent. Forest Park Addition was promoted as " . . . far superior to Vandeventer" and unlike Vandeventer it had the park as a permanent buffer.[10] It was laid out with two streets running east to west, each in turn divided by a landscaped median strip; one cross street was placed west of center. As originally allocated the lots were 100 feet wide and 195 feet deep, though some were later combined.[11]

The Steedmans' house at 34 Westmoreland was designed by Mauran, Russell & Garden, a prominent local firm.[12] A tepid rendition of the Prairie Style then flourishing under the leadership of Frank Lloyd Wright, the house had three stories and was constructed of brick with a plaster frieze below the eaves (Fig. 2.3). It probably is best interpreted as a reflection of Steedman's conservative instincts, especially in relation to many grander houses in the neighborhood. It probably was completed in 1910.[13]

George Steedman was a tireless worker; his accomplishments radiate intelligence. Foremost a mechanical engineer—he received forty-four patents between 1894 and 1921 for inventions ranging from elevators, hoists, and compressors to car brakes and a shingle-sawing machine—his interests expanded later to include architecture,

27

Fig. 2.2: Katherine, Medora, and George Steedman, ca. 1913.

metalworking, and wine making. He effectively retired from active participation in the affairs of Curtis & Company in 1919, assuming the title of vice president while his brother Edwin took over as president.[14] Though he was diagnosed with dilatation of the arch of the aorta in 1922, he continued to challenge others to meet his physical and mental agility.[15]

Like many of his ilk, Steedman was quietly philanthropic, in general leaving his mark without fanfare. He did allow his name to be used when he established a traveling fellowship at the School of Architecture, Washington University, and again when he and his wife donated a collection of books on architecture to the St. Louis Public Library.

In 1925 Steedman and Virginia Weddell, widow of Steedman's brother Harrison and by then wife of the American consul-general to Mexico City, founded the James Harrison Steedman Memorial Fellowship in Architecture at Washington University. It was " . . . established in the belief that travel in foreign lands will help to develop leaders in the practice or teaching of architecture, and particularly in the hope that it may promote architectural progress in St. Louis and its vicinity." The initial fund was $30,000 with provision for an annual award of $1,500. With the exception of interruptions resulting from global turmoil—the Depression and World War II—and occasional inadequate submissions, the Steedman Fellowship has been awarded regularly since. Probably the most prominent recipient was George F. Hellmuth, who won the fellowship in 1930 and was founding partner of Hellmuth, Obata & Kassabaum, a large architectural firm still operating today.[16]

The George Fox Steedman Architectural Collection at the St. Louis Public Library was established in November 1928. Steedman made his initial overture two years earlier, in October 1926, explaining that he was " . . . collecting a selected, representative, library on architecture and allied applied arts in connection with the Steedman Memorial Traveling Fellowship in Architecture — which has been endowed at Washington University." The collection was " . . . limited to books of an inspirational character to students and practitioners of architecture" that were selected " . . . from their value as to developing better architectural work in St. Louis." The volumes were " . . . of the character not usually found in the 'working libraries' of practicing architects . . . " and consisted " . . . primarily of old, rare or out of print, or foreign books—" Steedman inquired if the library board would accept the collection as an "outright gift" together with an endowment of $10,000 for "accretions and renewals," accrued income only to be spent. Steedman also offered a second $10,000 allocation toward construction of a "Memorial Room, alcove or balcony in your Art Room, provided your architects could work out a mutually satisfactory plan."[17] The board accepted the offer as it was outlined pending " . . . a satisfactory agreement regarding the installation."[18]

Mauran, Russell & Crowell, the firm responsible for the Steedmans' house on Westmoreland Place, is the architect of record for the new room although the actual design may be the work of a staff member, Oscar Mullgardt.[19] Steedman seems to have made no attempt to impose his newfound Spanish taste on Cass Gilbert's original 1912 building. J. L. Mauran, writing to his client on February 16, 1928, while the plans were in progress, described the room as " . . . pleasantly domestic (and in the best English tradition) . . . " He also noted that the board had authorized an appropriation of $10,000 from library funds toward construction.[20]

In fact, the $20,000 allocated jointly by Steedman and the library was inadequate—the room was elaborately and beautifully detailed—and by late 1928 the cost was estimated at $35,000. Steedman took care of the shortfall, agreeing to contribute up to $25,000. The final drawings are dated January 26, 1929, and show the room essentially as it was constructed; it opened in April 1930. A contemporary observer saw the addition as " . . . an intimate, charming small room that might be the private library of a cultured home" (Fig. 2.4). Steedman described it later as " . . . about 25 ft. square, entirely lined with books . . . ."[21]

When Steedman began the collection, he indicated his intention to work " . . . in a leisurely way, so as to try to do the work well and with the greatest amount of benefit and pleasure to myself."[22] The result was an exceptionally high-minded selection of approximately six hundred books and folios including seminal works on the theoretical and formal evolution of Western architecture to the nineteenth century. While the integrity of Steedman's gift cannot be questioned, his biases are clear. Modern architecture is ignored, even technological innovation which seemingly would have appealed.

There was one other substantial endowment in addition to numerous small annual donations. In 1930 Steedman established a $10,000 fund at Massachusetts General Hospital for heart research. Paul Dudley White, who gained prominence later as a consultant when President Dwight Eisenhower suffered a heart attack during his second term in office, began treating Steedman there in 1929. White explained in 1931 that a portion of the money had been used for installation of a new electrocardiograph and for professional assistance but that a substantial balance remained. By 1934 the fund had been reduced to less than $500; at White's behest Steedman added $500 but it was finally depleted in 1937.[23]

If not among the ranks of the very rich, Steedman clearly was extremely comfortable financially in the 1920s. The gifts to Washington University and the St. Louis Public Library were contemporary with the building and furnishing of his new house in Santa Barbara. In 1928 he made notes for a codicil revealing his wish to bequeath handsome gifts of money totaling several hundred thousand dollars to Harvard University and, in St. Louis, to Christ Church Cathedral and St. Luke's and Barnes Hospitals.[24]

At the same time, Steedman frequently expressed a desire for modesty in conduct and appearance, though there also was a propensity for occasional opulent display, nowhere better revealed than in newspaper accounts of his daughters' debutante parties and weddings. Katherine

was presented to society in 1925; the event was described as " . . . one of the most elaborate of the debut balls in the St. Louis Country Club." Her 1928 wedding gave "St. Louis society one of its most important early summer events and one of the loveliest of this season's weddings."[25] Medora's marriage in 1930 was "conspicuous among the important society events of the late autumn period" and, as for her sister, the press was effusive in reporting the elaborate wedding gowns and decorations at 34 Westmoreland.[26]

Fig. 2.3: Steedman house, St. Louis.

Fig. 2.4: George Fox Steedman Architectural Collection, St. Louis Public Library.

CHAPTER 3

Creating Casa del Herrero

Decorated ceilings and polychrome tiles . . . form the principal elements
of the Spanish house . . . all that is left is to put a wall between them.[1]

George and Carrie Steedman may first have visited Santa Barbara together in January 1921 when they accompanied his brother Harrison who had come to be treated for severe diabetes by Dr. William David Sansum, a pioneering specialist. They remained until Harrison's death on July 1, leasing a house adjoining his on Ashley Road (Fig. 3.1).[2]

The Steedmans returned to Santa Barbara the following year, 1922, this time renting a house on the southeast corner of Hot Springs Avenue (as it was then known) and Valley Road. One of the earliest Andalusian buildings in Santa Barbara, recent research confirms that James Osborne Craig was the architect (Fig. 3.2).[3] One wonders if Steedman was aware of this, and if the house influenced his decision to hire George Washington Smith.

Steedman soon purchased a seven-acre site on Valley Road within walking distance of the Craig house; the deed was recorded in mid-April 1922. The land was part of the acreage first subdivided in the nineteenth century as pueblo land grants and had been reallocated and sold several times. A contour map completed in March 1922 by F. F. Flournoy, a civil engineer, showed that the site was roughly trapezoidal and dropped off sharply to the south (Fig. 3.3). Two creeks meandered through and the ocean was on the horizon. Both Flournoy's map and a 1918 Sanborn map indicate an approximately fourteen-by-twenty-foot adobe structure roughly in the location of the present octagonal pool in the front courtyard. There were acacia, cypress, pepper, eucalyptus, and gum trees on the site as well as a stand of cactus.[4]

The choice of site invites questions. Valley Road was the principal east-west thoroughfare in Montecito, and there would seem to have been a relative lack of privacy, especially in comparison with Ashley Road. Also there was an assemblage of humble commercial buildings including the Montecito Store and the Montecito Home Club at the nearby San Ysidro Road intersection. In the same vein, remnants of an earlier era can be seen today at the intersection of East Valley Road and Cota Lane. Still, the site with its physical attributes and views of the mountains to the north and ocean to the south was undeniably impressive.

By May, Steedman had commissioned Smith to design the house. Steedman never explained his choice but his options were limited and speculation is easy. Craig suffered from asthma and had been staying in Ojai since October 1921 because of the drier climate. He died there at thirty-two the following March.[5] Of the remaining small group of architects working in Santa Barbara, few names provoke recognition today. Winsor Soule arrived in 1910 from his native New York and in 1921 formed a partnership with John F. Murphy and T. Mitchell Hastings. He became interested in Spanish architecture and traveled through Spain between February and July 1922. On his return he predicted, " . . . California will develop a new type of architecture retaining the old Spanish ideals in a simplified adaptation . . . ."[6] He followed up in December with a lecture based on the trip that was attended by more than one thousand people and a book, *Spanish Farmhouses and Minor Public Buildings*, published in 1924.[7]

Floyd E. Brewster (1888–1971), another New Yorker, had migrated to Santa Barbara by 1918. Though the circumstances are elusive, he was commissioned to design the new Hazard Memorial/Museum of Comparative Oology in Mission Canyon—later the Santa Barbara Museum of Natural History—that was dedicated in April 1922.[8]

This high-profile project seemingly was a professional dead end, at least temporarily, for he began working in Smith's office in January 1923, where he soon met George Steedman.[9]

Three other architects—Bertram Goodhue, whose own embellished adobe cottage, La Cabaña, was across Valley Road from the Casa site; Carleton Winslow; and Reginald Johnson—though not based in Santa Barbara, should be mentioned. All worked in the area frequently with clients financially and socially comparable to Steedman. While each would have seemed to be an obvious choice, there is no record of contact.

At the same time Steedman hired Smith, he also engaged Ralph Stevens to develop the site and design the garden. Ralph Tallant Stevens (1882–1958) was the son and spiritual heir of Ralph Kinton Stevens who developed Tanglewood, now called Lotusland, as a nursery in the late nineteenth century. The younger Stevens had a degree in landscape design from Michigan State University and worked with Peter Riedel, a landscape gardener, when the grounds at Tanglewood were renovated ca. 1919–20 for E. Palmer Gavit.[10] He served between 1919 and 1921 as park superintendent for the City of Santa Barbara, and Stevens Park was named after him.[11]

Casa del Herrero Estate was designed and built over a three-year period, 1922 to 1925. Many hands were involved, principally those of Smith and Steedman but also of Stevens; Lutah Maria Riggs, a 1919 graduate of the architecture program at the University of California, Berkeley, who was working in Smith's office; Brewster; Byne; and Carrie Steedman, though there is scant record of her input. Steedman established his working relationship with Smith early on, commenting that he was ". . . prone to make many suggestions, but also not at all prejudiced in favor of my individual ideas if I can find better ones. . . . "[12] Steedman indeed was not pen-shy, and Smith seemed generally amenable to the dialogue.

Steedman was a self-assured and assertive, though unfailingly polite, client. Although he was rarely in Santa Barbara while the designs were being formulated, his extensive correspondence reveals that he left nothing to chance. His letters, often accompanied by sketches, are rife with suggestions and minute detail. While he routinely told Smith to use his own good judgment, Smith frequently accepted Steedman's ideas. In fact, so many of the details were worked out by Steedman that Smith was to some extent reduced to the role of facilitator. Still, the resulting house was a collaboration of the best possible kind. A superior result was achieved that

would not have been possible without the mutual involvement.

Three undated and presumably preliminary schemes by Smith, numbered 1, 2, and 3, are two-story plans organized linearly with the principal rooms linked by an outdoor loggia. This layout was not developed further. The final design evolved in four distinct stages: the basic scheme appears in drawings dated May 1922 that were revised in June. The principal changes were in the location of the second-floor porch and the expression of the main stair as a semi-circular tower on the north elevation.

Steedman responded with his own plans in September followed by a counter proposal from Smith showing the main stair in the entrance hall and the entry itself on the diagonal through an octagonal

Fig. 3.1: 47 Ashley Road, Montecito.

Fig. 3.2: 136 Hot Springs Avenue.

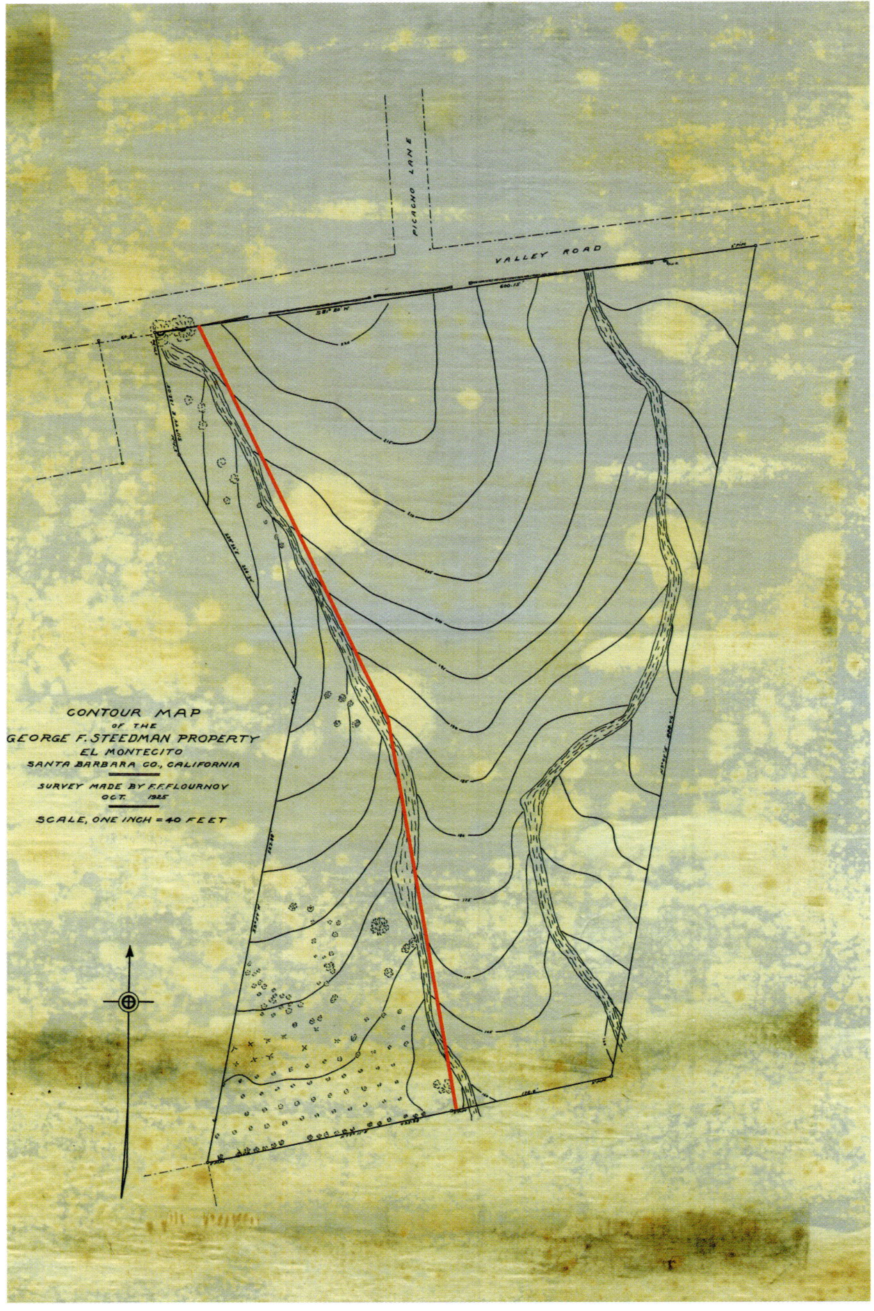

Fig. 3.3: F. F. Flournoy, contour map of the George F. Steedman Property, El Montecito, Santa Barbara Co., California. October 1925. The superimposed red line distinguishes the property Steedman acquired in 1922 from the smaller parcel he added in 1925.

ber 1922. The basic scheme is a combination of formal garden, orchard, and wilderness. Two entrances from Valley Road lead to a circular drive in front of the house and a major axis extends to the south in response to the obvious orientation. The axis is defined by hedges and terminates in a small pool and an existing pepper tree to which another was added to create a pair. Cactus—shown on Flournoy's survey—is indicated to the south. A walled "private garden" opens from the living room and a cutting garden bisected with paths extends beyond to the east. A "palm jungle" lines the eastern creek.

Stevens explained that "Nothing rare or scarce is called for, just good standard plant material . . . ." He continued that if Steedman did " . . . not particularly like the idea of giving the so-called Mexican or Arizona touch to the planting at the front entrance, I suggest the large-leaved semi-tropical character. This consists of Aralias, Bird of Paradise, Dracaena Treeferns [*sic*] etc. and many flowering things. . . ."[14]

Steedman responded with three detailed alternative suggestions based on the initial proposal which he labeled A, B and C; the structure of the garden in its earliest incarnation is here. His drawings contain extensive notes including an acknowledgment of ignorance about the "fundamentals of good landscape gardening . . . ."[15] He felt that Scheme <u>C</u> was ". . . far superior to any scheme yet suggested–it is simpler, stronger–less confused, and much easier to maintain, and is capable of enlargement in future if larger orchard wanted–and much more nearly conforms to my original idea of a small, simple <u>California</u> place 'by the road'." He intended to cultivate only a small portion of the overall site and had in mind that "One gardener is supposed to easily handle garden, wash car, and do janitor work . . . ." He added, "If I show too much planting for 1 man as above, then the amount of planting must be reduced . . . I . . . insist on 'one man' place after the planting is established."[16]

Water historically has been difficult to obtain in Montecito. Steedman's source was a well not on the estate but across Valley Road on property owned by Lyde V. Conrad. A water tower constructed there between October and early December 1922 was the first building completed; presumably it was based on one drawing in Smith's archive showing a tank supported on an open framework. Steedman purchased water from Mrs. Conrad's Carmelita Springs Water Company until 1927 when he acquired the property and replaced the tower with a new structure.

rather than circular tower. Drawings dated October 3 indicate the first floor plan essentially as it was constructed: the stair is incorporated into the volume of the house without expression on the facade. Throughout the design phase several locations were proposed for the second-floor sleeping porch; its final position is established in a plan of November 25. Another plan by Steedman dated December 30 includes the note "This is a final–approved study–<u>no</u> <u>changes</u> of any kind to be made unless except obvious errors–or of <u>trivial</u> character."[13] In fact, numerous refinements were on the horizon.

The first clue to Stevens's intentions for the Casa garden was a layout he sent to Steedman in Novem-

A cottage for the gardener was the second building undertaken; both Smith and Steedman attempted preliminary designs, neither to Steedman's liking. Smith's was a rectangular two-bedroom plan to which Steedman responded:

> Very pleasing artistically-but has adverse criticisms . . . . Living room is needlessly large . . . . House looks like a "villa" rather than a Spanish peasant house-I think "Spanish peasant house" most appropriate to the site . . . . Big open fireplace expensive and not usable by average gardener with wood @ $28.00 to $30.00 a cord . . . .[17]

Steedman's proposal, dated December 1922, included a bedroom for a chauffeur above the garage, an idea that reappeared in the final plan.

Smith's final scheme of February 1923 was designed shortly after a trip to Mexico he and his wife took with Riggs; a penciled annotation on one drawing notes that the Valley Road elevation is "à la Cuernavaca, Mexico."[18] The most inventive feature is the manner in which the two-story garage-bedroom unit was rotated a few degrees, distinguishing the gardener's quarters from the chauffeur's. The bathroom positioned between the living room and garage served as a hinge for the change in angle (Fig. 3.4). Steedman responded, " . . . I like your gardners [sic] cottage far better than my own suggestions–mine had no particular charm or appropriateness–your design has both to a marked degree–"[19]

Construction on the cottage began in February 1923 and while Smith wrote in July that it was "practically finished," work continued until September (Fig. 3.5). It was first occupied in December by John Hartfeld (1893–1965) who had been employed as gardener by Stevens on Steedman's behalf, and his family.[20]

In March 1923 Steedman wrote to Smith that he was " . . . again working over interior & exterior studies of residence, elevations and details–all purely tentative–to help develop details promptly . . . . I shall forward same to you from time to time for your criticism and revision so that I can have the full benefit of your advice." Commenting in another letter two days later that he had "been dissatisfied with the den for some time," Steedman reworked it repeatedly before eliminating it altogether and incorporating the space allocated to it into the living room.[21]

The planning process was both dependent on and delayed by a trip to Spain that Steedman took in 1923 to buy furniture, decorative arts, and architectural fragments for the new house. The trip occurred in May and June; Louis La Beaume, an architect friend from St. Louis, accompanied him. La Beaume (1873–1961) had designed several houses—though not Steedman's—in Westmoreland/Portland Place, where Steedman lived, and also had published a book on Mexican architecture in 1915 based on a trip the previous year.[22] They disembarked May 14 in Cherbourg and went immediately to Paris; from there they made their way to Madrid via Biarritz, Burgos and Segovia over a five-day period on the Sud Express (Fig. 3.6).

In Madrid they met with Byne and Mildred Stapley, whose scholarly pursuits had been derailed, to some extent, by entrepreneurial instincts, as Stapley explained to her friend Julia Morgan:

> Knowing, as we now do, the charm of the traditional Spanish house we envy you architects of California your opportunity to create something fine in this line . . . . Meanwhile, if we can't build Spanish residences, we can furnish them. Our opportunities for disposing of good old private collections were so numerous that it seemed a pity not to take advantage of them, so we have become antiquarios [sic].[23]

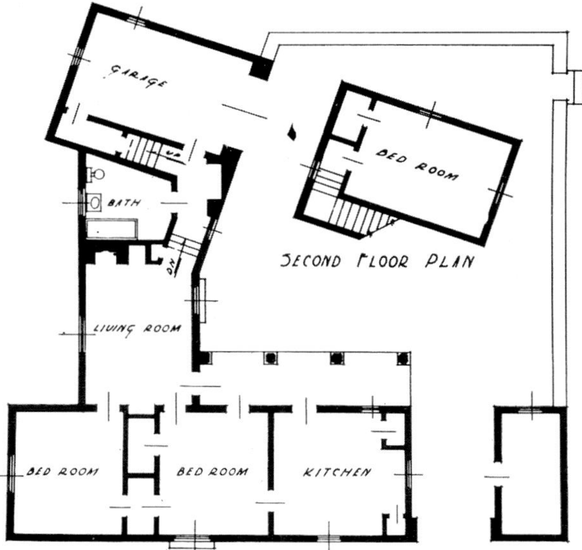

Fig. 3.4: Gardener's cottage, plan.

Fig. 3.5: Gardener's cottage, north elevation.

35

The Bynes served as "guides and counsillors [*sic*]" on a seven-week "furniture and fitting hunt in Spain" interspersed with visits to significant landmarks and private collections. Steedman took some three thousand photographs along the way, which he later sent to Smith for reference; he also sketched and made notes. After returning, La Beaume published his account of the expedition

Fig. 3.6: George Steedman, Segovia, May 1923.

FACING PAGE TOP
Fig. 3.7: Arthur Byne and George Steedman, measured detail sketch, Generalife, Granada, June, 1923.

FACING PAGE BOTTOM
Fig. 3.8: Spanish garden from cutting garden.

in a series of articles collectively entitled "A Little Tour in Spain." It's a high-minded tale of cultural exploration and discovery but La Beaume occasionally allowed incidents of intrepidness cushioned by deep pockets to creep in. Primarily they were at the mercy of the Spanish trains, which, La Beaume noted, "simply do not correlate."[24]

They first went to Toledo where among many sites they visited the Casa y Museo de El Greco, which Byne had seen in 1910 and written about the following year, suggesting it as a prototype for contemporary building. Steedman sketched several details, notably the entry steps that became the

prototype for the stairs leading to the Spanish garden from the Casa living room.

The group returned to Madrid the next day and began shopping. Invoices reveal Steedman's innate decisiveness: in one day he acquired ironwork; doors; all but one of the tables in the Casa; several chairs; chests and cabinets including the *vargueño* (Spanish cabinet) in the living room and decorative items. The next day they visited the residences of the Conde de las Almenas and the Duchess Parcent before leaving for Lisbon. Information about activities in Lisbon is limited to Steedman's cryptic notes: "drove and saw shops." There is no record of purchases.[25]

The trip from Lisbon to Seville involved a change in plans, as La Beaume recounted:

> We had come from Badajoz, on the Portuguese frontier, in a Ford . . . . We hadn't intended coming to such an ancient city in such a new Ford, or even in any Ford, but had missed connections at Badajoz and were not enamoured enough of the Fonda where we made our breakfast to tarry there. So we bargained for the car, which had evidently just been uncrated, found a youth to drive it, roped our baggage to the running boards [and] rattled across the bridge and out along the old Roman road . . . though our chauffeur had never been so far away as Seville, he seemed for a while on familiar ground and always on familiar terms with the Camineros, or road builders, from whom we were frequently obliged to beg water for our thirsty mechanism . . . .
>
> We made but one more stop, and that involuntarily, until we were halted at the douane on the outskirts of Seville. Our chariot had taken water again some miles back and we were tripping along just at twilight . . . . Suddenly at the foot of what seemed a towering mountain we stopped. We had gas—a little—but the grade was too steep, and it wouldn't flow . . . . Our lad was embarrassed, chagrined, mortified. We looked at the white line of road zog-zagging its way toward the stars and wondered if we dared the perilous experiment of backing to the top. Wracked with impotence and indecision, we spied another car far up making its winding descent. It came nearer and nearer. Its occupants bowed and stopped. Our boy seemed to know the driver as he had known the Camineros and, the passengers acquiescing, in a moment we had performed the operation of gasoline transfusion and with "*muchas gracias*" oft repeated, and many bows to our saviours, were on our way.[26]

Andalusia was a Spain different from what Steedman had seen before and one architecturally more relevant to his undertaking in Santa Barbara because of the specific regional idiom. In Seville they visited the Alcazar garden with its tiled Pavilion of Charles V and two of the great houses, Casa de Pilatos and Casa de las Dueñas, both displaying extensive tile work. They also witnessed the medieval festival of Corpus Christi with its procession and theatrical performances. La Beaume described "Rugs, banners, great cloths of damask or velvet, even bright bedspreads [hanging] from every balcony . . ." and a "stir of excitement everywhere."[27]

They stayed in Seville for approximately nine days during which they ventured twice to Ronda and, inexplicably defying geographic logic, to Cordoba and back in one day. In Seville Steedman acquired several of the most prominently displayed items in the Casa, including the fine Mudejar seventeenth-century doors and frame for the second-floor hall, the sixteenth-century escutcheon over the living room fireplace, and the *reja* for the stair hall window, an important feature of the north facade. He also bought iron wall brackets and tin lanterns for very small amounts of money and three sets of "modern Sevillian painted furniture" for the servants' bedrooms.

The last stop in Andalusia was Granada, the final stronghold of the Moors before it fell to the Catholics Ferdinand and Isabella in January 1492. It was there that Muslim architecture reached its climax in the fourteenth-century Alhambra whose unsurpassed sculptural decoration belies its function as a hilltop fortress. More useful to Steedman, however, were the gardens of the Generalife, a summer palace nearby. La Beaume found them "simple yet intricate, naïve but profoundly sophisticated."[28] Byne and Steedman measured and sketched one of the arcaded walls; this was the prototype for the enclosed Spanish garden at the Casa (Figs. 3.7, 3.8).

The travelers returned to Madrid from Granada, then went to Barcelona where they remained June 14 to 18, shopping every day. The Martyrdom of St. Lorenzo now hanging in the Casa dining room was the most significant purchase. Writing from Barcelona, Steedman described his accomplishments to Smith:

> Our purchases have either been made, or arrangements made to complete same after my departure–and arrangements are under way for marking–listing–packing–and shipping–a big job. Apparently we will have to ship via N.Y. in bond for L.A. –but that is not definitely settled . . . .
>
> It is arranged that Mr. Byne will send direct to you . . . all consular invoices and shipping documents for all California shipments—and you will please . . . make your local arrangements for passing through customs, forwarding to Santa Barbara, and storage . . . .
>
> Mr. Byne and Mr. La Beaume are quite satisfied with purchases made up to date–and I am enthusiastic

Fig. 3.9: Arthur Byne,
Sketch for Tile, Tunis,
January 1924.

Fig. 3.10: Tile, Les Fils
de J. Chemla, Tunis.

over same–Some of the items are–a XV century genuine painted wooden ceiling for front hall – a splendid Mudejar door and frame about 6' x 8' for the 2nd floor hall–just about the mass you indicated in your sketch – numerous other good doors and shutters–more rejas than I can use, and some of them very good–some carved corbels–good iron details–and most primitive Gothic paintings and hangings. I hope you will find them interesting– We still have Mallorca ahead of us–I sail from Liverpool June 29th.[29]

As indicated, Byne continued to make purchases for the Casa after Steedman left. In September he negotiated the acquisition of two tapestries from a dealer in Paris, a French Mille Fleur hunting scene and a Flemish depiction of an Old Testament episode. At $10,000 for the pair these were by far Steedman's costliest purchases. Byne praised them in a letter to Smith: "I am sure you will like the tapestries bought in Paris for Mr. Steedman, particularly the mille-fleur which combined with the XV-century painted ceiling ought to create a really imposing entrance hall."[30]

Byne injected mild humor into the pursuit of a group of *fraileros* (chairs) from a convent in Palma, reporting " . . . a lively correspondence with the newly appointed Mother Superior . . . . The old ladies can't make up their minds whether or not they wish to part with the chairs." Two weeks later, they did " . . . by raising the price to 120 pesetas apiece."[31]

It fell to Byne as well to orchestrate the shipments from Spain to Santa Barbara; initially there were eighty-seven cases but many more were on the horizon. Smith, far exceeding his role as architect, agreed to take over on the receiving end, coordinating with Wheeler, Elder & Elder, customs brokers in Los Angeles, and arranging for transport to Santa Barbara. Writing to Smith about the details, Byne stated that he was " . . . trying to make clear . . . the contents of the various boxes so as to minimize the packing and unpacking in California." He also made clear that he had found a soul mate in Steedman:

Mr. Steedman we found most delightful. It is the first time that we ever consented to conduct a visitor around Spain, for between our books and the sale of antiques, our time is very much taken up, still the trip could hardly have been more enjoyable. Mr. Steedman is a prodigious worker and dreadfully in earnest about his house (as you probably well know) so that every moment was taken up . . . .

It is rare indeed that one has the opportunity of working with such an intelligent and enthusiastic client.[32]

Steedman and his family spent the summer of 1923 in Northeast Harbor, Maine. He wrote from there to George Washington Smith that he expected to see him in the middle of September and that there was " . . . no hurry in having any conference on the house plans until the Spanish purchases arrive."[33]

At about this time, Steedman proposed a name for the house, explaining his rationale to Smith:

"Herrero"–according to the Spanish dictionary is "Smith"–You are a Smith, I am a smith so I believe Casa del Herrero is the appropriate name for the house–

He discussed the idea with Byne as well, who responded:

. . . we think <u>Casa del Herrero</u> is capital. Don't forget; the H is silent and the R's rolled with a good Scotch burr.[34]

Steedman also addressed the need to obtain tile for the Casa. He had purchased a limited number of antique tiles and larger quantities of modern Sevillian tile but needed much more (Fig. 3.13). He explained that he " . . . did not have sufficient time in Spain to study the modern tile market–what I saw led me to believe that it was very difficult to find good modern Spanish tile–but that it may be possible to find some small manufacturer who <u>makes</u> and decorates his tile by hand . . ." and indicated that he was writing to Byne, asking him to try to locate such a tile maker. He concluded, "The more I saw of old and new tiles in Spain the surer I became that we should use but <u>very</u> <u>little</u> tile . . . ."[35]

Smith responded, " . . . the only tile I have ever found that I can use satisfactorily other than antique tile, is a tile made in Tunis by, I understand, an old Spanish family, made by hand." He was referring to the firm Les Fils de J. Chemla and later suggested that Byne arrange to purchase this tile. Steedman did not at first accept this suggestion, writing on August 24 that he had samples of the Tunis tile and felt " . . . almost certain Mr. Byne can get as good or better tile in Spain at a small fraction of the cost . . . ." On September 10, Byne wrote to Smith, "Mr. Steedman is much concerned over tiles for his house (as he has every reason to be). I am frankly not in favor of modern Spanish tiles; I am sure more artistic results can be had in America for less money. As to the Tunis Tiles I have never seen any but have often heard them praised. Of course old Spanish tiles, to my mind, are always preferable but difficult to obtain in uniform quantities." Byne followed up two days later in a letter to Steedman stating, " . . . I will gladly undertake anything I can in connection with the Casa del Herrero so

Fig. 3.11: Arthur Byne, Sketch for Tile, Tunis, January 1924.

Fig. 3.12: Tile, Les Fils de J. Chemla, Tunis.

Fig. 3.13: Fireplace detail, George Steedman bedroom.

far as tiles are concerned" although there was no immediate action.[36]

Steedman met with Smith in Santa Barbara in late September to go over the house plans and review the photographs he had taken in Spain. There is little information about dialogue that took place during this visit but the upshot seems to have been that Steedman revised the existing drawings himself. On November 5 he wrote to Smith that he was sending the latest study of the ground floor, dated November 1; the second-floor plan followed on November 30.[37] These drawings have not been located; however, they must have led to detailed studies showing placement of the Spanish purchases that Steedman sent the next month.

By this time problems with the shipments from Spain had become apparent. The process was fraught with cultural differences—the Spanish mentality described by Byne was at odds with American expectations—and, later, transportation strikes and political chicanery. American bureaucratic intervention compounded the inherently tedious process. The first shipment left Seville in

June; shipments from Barcelona, Granada, and Madrid followed in early July.[38]

The confusion became apparent with the arrival of the shipment from Seville in October, as Smith described: "The trouble seems to be that the cases are not numbered properly, if numbered at all . . . . Then the actual articles are not tagged or numbered . . . and on the other hand some of the cases contain articles not invoiced at all . . . ." Smith summarized in November in a letter to Byne: " . . . out of a clear blue sky 29 or 65 or 48 cases arrive in Los Angeles from somewhere."[39]

Byne responded twice. First he told Steedman " . . . the Spanish packers and shippers are absolutely irresponsible and would make mistakes that we would think impossible." He followed up a month later with the information that the shipper " . . . merely addressed his invoice to 'Jorge Steedman, California'" and concluded wryly, "I doubt if you have had time to become quite so well known in that state." While Smith's correspondence reveals the great extent of his involvement, Steedman's sympathy was with Byne and " . . . the amount of work that poor man has been to in handling my purchases."[40]

Anticipating another meeting with Smith in January, Steedman acknowledged that the trip to Spain and the complications of having his purchases shipped to Santa Barbara had caused the long delay but now he was ready to move ahead. He was hoping to " . . . concentrate on details and finally get the house plans so that you can finish the building without a lot of long correspondence between us." Smith responded, " . . . I hope . . . to have the plans in shape for discussion."[41]

In the interim, Byne asked for a list of tile that would be needed " . . . so that I can get it going in the works here." Smith sent the list in December, again holding out for Tunisian tile. Steedman gave Byne full " . . . discretion and authority . . . " to select the tile with the reminder, " . . . I want to keep things simple and don't want to do anything needlessly extravagant, and I always try to lean toward the simple, conservative thing rather than the highly organized or showy."[42]

Byne and Stapley went to Tunis in January 1924 to obtain the tile. The process took on a life of its own, as Stapley reported:

> Fourth day in Tunis . . . . Don't advise it as a winter resort to yr. friends unless they be archaeologists who want to study the excavations at Carthage; or are prepared to adore . . . Arab dirt & disease . . . .
>
> Imagine how our hopes were dashed on finding Chemla ill; we were left to ramble over his pottery works–a mere yard where a number of Arabs are working in the same primitive manner that you saw at Fajalanfa outside Granada . . . .
>
> We picked out the tiles whose design most approached the Spanish, had a large basket of them brought to the hotel, & have since been laying the floor of our room in a thousand different schemes. The designs are not exactly what we hoped to encounter, but the technique surpasses everything in Spain . . . .
>
> As foreseen, Chemla . . . had never seen a blue print. The array of them frightened him. Of all that was explained to him he seized but one motif: being an Oriental he took immediately to the idea of making a fountain. In fact . . . we begin to fear that nothing else will be done till the little garden embellishment is turned out to his satisfaction!
>
> Never mind, we are going to see it through . . . . A. is making drawings day & night, explicit down to the last detail, all numbered & lettered in French according to the specimens we have selected.[43]

Five days later, Byne reported that he had " . . . just this minute terminated with M. Chemla . . . . We have gone into the question of the tiles for the Casa del Herrero in a most exhaustive manner." He continued:

> My wife wrote you of some of the difficulties we were experiencing: the truth is we could never begin to tell you all the troubles we have had. To begin with, let me say that a hand-made product in a land like ours, for example, very much assisted by every known mechanical appliance is a very different thing from a hand-made product in Africa where nothing else but a primitive tradition is known . . . .
>
> And now as to the decorative quality of the tiles: they are very beautiful but our task was made extremely difficult for the reason that there is no stock to draw from . . . . Fortunately for us there is a most excellent museum of old Persian and Tunisian tiles and with these before me I was able to design a sufficient number of patterns. I made full size drawings of all these with color-notes and in each case referring definitely to the old example from wh. I copied (Figs. 3.9–3.12). There is no doubt in my mind about Chemla's ability to reproduce these as all the chemical side of the work has long been the family patrimony and they can secure most artistic results . . . .
>
> Another difficulty was that all Chemla's tiles, like the Persian they follow, have the various patterns outlined by a dark line of manganese wh. keep the colors from running to-gether: now this is contrary to the Spanish tradition and in some cases very bad. . . . I worked days with Chemla to convince him of this. Now he can do it and is enthusiastic over the thought. At the same time I didn't dare try the experiment in very important places. So you see, in many ways, I was much held

down by local traditions – wh. are of a pottery nature more than architectonic.

Still I am confident you will receive a stack of excellent tiles . . . . [44]

Another letter from Byne written a week later reveals his intentions. "Have created a stair in black and green, I think very effective. I am not so sure about the advisability of the dado, think twice before doing it as it is apt to rob the stair walls of their simplicity. For my taste the black 'scrub' will suffice . . . . Worked very hard over the dressing room and lavatory. Tried for black and silver scheme but Chemla wasn't sure of himself. Smith's scheme in blue and white alone I felt would be cheerless. My scheme is much more colorful–blue, green, yellow, and white . . . . Baths gave me much to worry over and will worry you still . . . . You must simplify the panel forms and regulate heights. Much of the success here depends on the colors Chemla secures particularly the apple green." Byne concluded: "This Tunisian tile is going to be a 'great adventure.' If they turn out well I should like to be around–if not, well . . . ."[45]

By January 1924 Steedman had become hesitant about going to Santa Barbara and told Smith candidly: "I do not think it will pay me to make a special trip to California until you have the Spanish shipments properly and conveniently warehoused or stored, and some of your more important studies have progressed to a point where we can finally settle all necessary details . . . ." Steedman also addressed ongoing frustration with Stevens. In November he had written to Stevens that he was " . . . still waiting . . . for detail sketches and plans for landscape work." A month later Steedman told Smith he was " . . . very much discouraged over Stevens' lack of attention and I fear that I may suffer considerable disappointment at his hands." Steedman's intuition was confirmed when Stevens sent " . . . sketches which I don't think are very satisfactory, and I have asked him to hold things up until I arrive before he does any actual work."[46]

Smith responded, "I have your first and second floor plans fairly well worked out as far as I can go with it, and will have the elevations and details you ask for by the time you arrive." Presumably this is a group of drawings dated January 18. Steedman met with his architect a short time later with the expressed intention of " . . . getting the house plans in such shape that you can go ahead without any further attention on my part."[47] He left, however, without the resolution he hoped for, particularly concerning the entrance hall.

Steedman proceeded to Los Angeles where he met with Marshall Laird, a cabinetmaker who spe-cialized in reproducing Spanish, Italian, and English furniture and who would fabricate pieces for the Casa; and B. B. Bell, a metalworker who electrified—and in some cases refinished—the lighting fixtures purchased in Spain. Steedman had seen their work in the new University Club in Los Angeles, designed by Allison and Allison, and was satisfied though he felt Laird had "surer taste." Laird also could " . . . fake age splendidly, and [do] fine work and good design."[48]

In early February Steedman met Carrie and Katherine at Castle Hot Springs, Arizona, an isolated desert resort they had visited in 1919. Located some fifty miles northwest of Phoenix, it opened in 1896—nearly two decades before the San Marcos Hotel in Chandler—as Arizona's first luxury resort but closed after a fire in 1976 and now is largely forgotten. While there, Steedman prepared tentative drawings for the walled or Spanish garden off the living room based on sketches made at the Generalife in Granada and for the entrance hall and sleeping porch. As usual, he encouraged Smith to use his own good judgment, to "Deviate all you please from my sketches until you get a result that satisfies you–"[49]

Steedman's many suggestions finally provoked a response on March 19 when Smith wrote, "The great problem has been to catch and assemble all the immense amount of detail we have received from you . . . ." Smith was referring not only to design issues but technical questions ranging from furnaces to kitchen appliances to servant call bells. Smith commented again in April that he felt the " . . . necessity of getting work started . . . but there has been, as you know, an immense amount of your notes and records to look up and alocate [*sic*], and the drawings have required an extraordinary amount of preparatory research work among the records, before progress could be made."[50]

Smith sent the revised plans in late April. Steedman responded that he was " . . . delighted with them, in general." Not dissuaded by time constraints, however, he returned them "with numerous notes." While some points could " . . . be considered as definitely settled," others required Smith's " . . . constructive criticism." The most significant issue was the entrance hall, which was not yet resolved to the Steedmans' satisfaction.[51]

On May 23, 1924, Smith informed Steedman that he had sent working drawings to Los Angeles to have blueprints made. He commented, " . . . they have been carried as far as they can at the present time, and . . . have been carried sufficiently far, to obtain estimates from Messrs. Snook & Kenyon . . . . This will at least allow construction on the building to start very shortly." He again noted the " . . .

tremendous amount of data that had to be incorporated into these drawings," and that it had taken approximately a month to complete them.[52]

Seeing the blueprints Steedman wrote back to Smith, "The house will be most satisfactory to me, and I hope will be good enough to give you some return for all the work which you have had to put on it." He continued, however, that he had ". . . been forced to the conclusion that there is not enough light in the front hall . . . " and " . . . it would be a rank mistake to have the hall, with its fine ceiling and tapestry, without any reasonable amount of daylight in it." At Smith's suggestion, Floyd Brewster stopped in St. Louis in June, en route back to Los Angeles from New York, to discuss the blueprints and Steedman's wish for further changes, though the subject of the hall was not resolved and would come up again.[53]

house without any further communication with me." In fact, between June 23 and 28 Steedman peppered Smith with numerous detailed letters and sketches and then concluded "I do not believe you will hear from my [*sic*] again until I return in October. I wish you the best of success and luck with the house, and I am not going to worry or think about it while I am away . . . ."[55]

If nothing else, Steedman was analytical and determined. Although he, Carrie, Katherine, and Medora sailed in early July, correspondence from him—and in his absence, his secretary—continued unabated. He acknowledged this, writing from the ocean liner Paris, " . . . I certainly fired in suggestions the last week I was home . . . ." And he again offered false hope of complacency in saying " . . . after a week of calm weather and plenty of leisure to think—that not a single thought or desire to

Fig. 3.14: Casa del Herrero under construction.

Smith received the Snook & Kenyon estimate on June 9 and forwarded it to Steedman who responded, "The house is going to be a very expensive one, I am afraid, but as I wrote you a few days ago, we have gone too far to make any changes in specifications or details and I am glad to trust your judgment to keep the cost of the house down as much as possible, commensurate with good common sense and good taste."[54]

In January Steedman had indicated his intention to spend the summer in Europe. On June 23, anticipating the trip, he gave Smith full license to complete the house " . . . on your own responsibility . . . making changes which you think are an improvement or correcting what you believe may be errors of taste or judgment on my part." He believed the blueprints and notes were complete and " . . . will enable you to go forward with the

change the house any further has come to me—and I hope the news may be tranquillizing to you . . . ."[56]

Smith responded to Steedman's "letter from the steamer" with "little sketches" for "an important change." He was addressing the undercurrent of mutual dissatisfaction with the entrance hall, correctly seen by both parties as the most important space in the house. Architect and client expressed themselves with uncharacteristic candor: Steedman cabled his rejection and Smith cabled back, " . . . regret your present decision." Both men followed up with letters, Smith explaining his objections and Steedman holding fast: " . . . I appreciate that I am assuming a great deal to contradict your best judgment . . . . I feel however . . . very strongly the wisdom of adhering to my floor plan . . . even to the extent of tearing down and rebuilding what may be necessary to carry out my ideas."[57]

43

Ultimately, Byne resolved the issue. He and Stapley joined the Steedmans at Tours and Steedman requested his advice. Steedman wrote to Smith, "Mr. Byne felt that the vestibule should be treated as far as possible as a part of the hall, and nothing done to accentuate its being separate. You will see from the floor plan and sketches that Mr. Byne's ideas for simplicity are even more positive than mine–" Smith responded, "I believe your solution of Hall treatment will be most satisfactory. You and Mr. Byne have solved a difficult condition . . . ."[58]

While in Florence, Steedman made additional purchases for the Casa including stone garden ornaments and the "Byzantine" door surround leading from the herb garden to the garage court. In Paris he acquired a carved wooden door removed from the sacristy of a church in Étretat, a resort town on the north coast of France. After buying it Steedman wrote to Smith, "The more I think over the door . . . the more I feel I may have stumbled on something good–"[59]

Steedman initially hoped the Casa would be completed by Christmas 1924 but by late October it was still an unenclosed shell (Fig. 3.14). In December Snook and Kenyon projected a more realistic date of June 15, 1925, explaining that the stone and tile work were necessarily slow. Hearing of the delay, Steedman wrote to Brewster: "On account of the house not being finished until June, Mrs. Steedman and I have made some very unexpected changes in our plans . . . . On April 1st we will sail for England for a six weeks' stay . . . ."[60]

In the interim the Steedmans took what Brewster called "side trips." First they went to Louisiana where they were the guests of E. A. McIlhenny, president of Tabasco, on his family's Avery Island, where the pepper sauce is made. Then they went to Mexico—to Tampico and Mexico City—where Steedman wrote to Smith that he was " . . . very much surprised and impressed with the architecture here–I wish I had brought my cameras along–" Smith responded, "There are a tremendous number of things you should see . . . ." In Mexico City he suggested that photographs " . . . at Cheurubusco [*sic*: Churubusco] . . . would be very valuable . . . Also, at San Angel there is a beautiful ceiling in the Sacristy of the Monestary [*sic*] . . . ." Smith further recommended the cathedrals at Cuernavaca and Guadalupe. He concluded, "Mexico is as fine as Spain in a great number of ways, maby [*sic*] more so-even."[61]

Steedman next made his way to Santa Barbara to meet with Smith and during this visit made one more significant change to the plans. As initially designed the north end of the living room was partitioned off as a den on the line of the beam overhead to the left as the room is entered. Several options for the dividing wall, some including a darkroom and storage, were proposed. In the end, the partition was not constructed. The arched alcove in the beauty parlor that was to have opened to the den remains as evidence of the original intention. The cabinet on the east wall of the living room now housing phonograph equipment was designed to hold firewood; when the rooms were combined, the carved sacristy door Steedman purchased in Paris in 1924 was hung there.

While in Santa Barbara Steedman also " . . . acceded to Miss Riggs logic as to placing of the watering trough"—an exedra that had been added on the far south horizon—and asked John Hartfeld to move an existing mockup to the new location which, as can be seen today, was notably off axis. On the way back to St. Louis in early March Steedman as usual " . . . kept busy on the train," dropping memos in the mail along the way and indicating that he could " . . . go to Europe and think no more of house details . . . ." All good intentions aside, during the three weeks he was in St. Louis Steedman dispatched no fewer than twenty-one letters to Smith.[62]

Writing again from the Plaza Hotel in New York on April 1, Steedman told Smith to "Please count on my arrival in Santa Barbara about June 15th, and the rest of the family July 1st–and I sincerely trust the house will be finished in ample time."[63]

Indeed, at the end of May 1925, Smith wrote to Steedman that the " . . . house in a general way is practically finished." He continued:

> I believe it is and will be considered the most successful house in the Montecito valley. I mean this, and have never said it before about any other house. I feel certain that you will be delighted with the result subject possibly to some minor details.

Steedman responded that he was " . . . greatly delighted, also greatly astonished, at your estimate of 'Casa del Herrero.' You have been a long-suffering martyr over this house, and you take a great weight off my conscience when you say that you believe it is successful."[64]

Steedman went to Santa Barbara in mid-June 1925 and reportedly stayed at the Santa Barbara Club on Chapala Street until " . . . odd items . . . " mentioned by Smith were completed. He first occupied the Casa on June 29, the day of the great Santa Barbara Earthquake, and memorialized the event in an inscription on a reworked sixteenth-century escutcheon over the fireplace in the living room (Fig. 3.15).[65] Carrie, Katherine, and Medora arrived a short time later.[66]

CASA DEL HERRERO
IS BUILT ON OUTER
PUEBLO LANDS OF SANTA BARBARA.
BOUGHT BY JOSE De JESUS COTA.
FOR NINETY TWO CENTS AN ACRE IN 1868.
TWENTY TWO YEARS AFTER GENERAL.
FREMONT CAPTURED THE TOWN PRESIDIO.
THIS HOUSE WAS FIRST OCCUPIED ON
THE MORNING OF THE GREAT EARTH
QUAKE, JUNE TWENTY NINTH 1925

CHAPTER 4

Playing Some More

George Steedman was an inveterate perfectionist. He made numerous alterations and additions to the house, beginning almost immediately. Lutah Maria Riggs accompanied the Steedmans on their three-day trip back to St. Louis in September 1925, talking over modifications. Steedman followed up with George Washington Smith, sending "memoranda and sketches . . . divid[ing] the work into logical groups . . . ." He concluded, "Please do not consider these numerous changes in any way evidencing any dissatisfaction with the house as it now is. We are thoroly [*sic*] pleased with it, and it is only because we like it so much that we want to play some more with it."[1]

Steedman wanted to bring the Casa to a level of precision more commonly associated with a feat of engineering than a Spanish farmhouse, and he wore his architect out in the process. He proposed deceptively simple changes that with hindsight seem finicky and could only have been interpreted as such at the time. Smith, polite in his initial written response, was less than aggressive in undertaking the work. Only under intensifying pressure from Steedman were some of the changes begun in November with Smith acknowledging, "I have taken a longer time than I should over these matters as I have been extremely busy . . . ."[2]

Most important was the replacement of wood frames and sash in the south dining room window, whose "stone work and general opening" Steedman found "so interesting," with much thinner steel "to show all that is possible of the opening." The three wood-framed windows were transferred to the shop and again to the new shop built in 1934, where they remain. At the same time the arched openings from the entry hall to the dining room and stair hall were reduced in both height and width; telltale evidence of this change is visible today.[3]

The earliest photographs of the newly completed Casa were published in 1926 and 1927. Three, taken by J. W. Collinge, a local photographer, are especially revealing. One shows the south elevation with its original loggia parapet and fountain, and living and bedroom windows as they appeared before the installation of antique surrounds purchased from Arthur Byne in 1927 (Fig. 4.1). The others reveal an arrangement of furniture in the living room very different to the one familiar today (Figs. 4.2, 4.3).[4]

Fig. 4.1: Casa, south elevation.

Fig. 4.2: Casa living room looking south.

Fig. 4.3: Casa living room looking north and showing the carved wooden door from the sacristy of a church in Étretat, France, later installed in the Book Tower, and the original corner fireplace.

No aspect of Casa del Herrero Estate was reworked more vigorously than the garden. It was problematic from the beginning. Steedman found the original design uninspired and Ralph Stevens unresponsive; he expressed dissatisfaction early on. In a letter to Smith in 1924 he commented, "I note that Mr. Stevens' bills are continuing to run about thirteen or fourteen hundred dollars a month. I hope he is about at the end of his expenditures." Steedman followed up with Stevens in the same vein, noting " . . . things look as though they must be nearing a satisfactory conclusion" while also expressing measured pique. With Stevens's photographs at hand he observed, "The entrance posts on either side of the main drive look fairly well, although I am sorry you did not follow more closely the texture and feeling of the photographs I sent you which show much smaller stones. Do not make any change, however, but let these stand as they now are." He was more "disappointed" in other gateways " . . . as they do not at all follow the Spanish photographs either as to shape or texture." Steedman sent " . . . instructions to request you to tear down this work and have it put in again in keeping with the style shown in my Spanish photographs which I gave to you . . . . Please give this matter your best attention, study the photographs carefully and try to get Hartfelt [*sic*] or whoever is going to do the work to use some good taste and make the work look Spanish when it is finished, not Welsh or Irish."[5]

Peter Riedel (1873–1954), a landscape gardener who worked on many local estates, may in fact have participated in some of this early work. A Dutch immigrant, he arrived in Santa Barbara in 1905. Much of his reputation rests on his association with the Southern California Acclimatizing Association founded by Francesco Franceschi, a Florentine horticulturist who is credited with introducing hundreds of exotic plants to Santa Barbara. The relationship with Franceschi ended in 1909. While various sources note but do not explain Riedel's involvement at the Casa, surviving invoices suggest that his tenure was brief and limited to providing building and plant materials and labor.[6]

Though disaffected, Steedman allowed Stevens to work through June 1925, asking Smith to " . . . keep after Mr. Stevens . . . " and commenting, " . . . I haven't found that he has any originality or artistic taste . . . ."[7] A nonetheless compelling drawing by Stevens (dated 1925 by Steedman) shows the garden as it was first laid out (Fig. 4.4). The major aspects of the 1922 plan—the two entrances and circular drive at the front, the axial extension to the south and the orchard—appear along with a third entry road near the gardener's cottage that snakes around the grounds and terminates in a path at the western property line. Another path loops through the southernmost part of the property, past the "Moorish watering trough." Overall the design is marked by its gradual transition from structured formality near the house to at least the *appearance* of undefiled nature in the distance. The result is a studied synthesis of gardens from different eras reflecting at once a contemporary point of view and a regional eclecticism which persists today.

Horticulturally the defining element was the orchard, primarily citrus but also including numerous other types of fruit trees and some fifty grape vines, which Steedman noted were not for winemaking.[8] Palms—notably the "palm jungle" of Canary Island date palms near the eastern creek but other species as well—were juxtaposed with conifers and large numbers of acacia and eucalyptus trees. There also were cacti and other succulents. A kitchen garden was planted in 1925 and although there were flowers, the cutting garden—identified on Stevens's plan and later to be a major feature—was not developed to any extent at this time.

Steedman began modifying the garden almost immediately, both enlarging it and incorporating new structural features. In 1925 he added approximately three acres to the southwest that included the western creek, which had been more or less bisected by the original property line (see Fig. 3.3, page 34).[9] The design changes occurred over several years and can be described generally though a strict chronology has not been established. The overall emphasis seems to have been on simplification and opening up of spaces.

Steedman seemingly approached Francis T. Underhill and Lockwood de Forest, Jr., about modifying the garden before he returned to St. Louis in September 1925. He followed up shortly in a letter to Smith saying that he hoped Smith and de Forest would " . . . co-operate and do whatever is necessary for the best results." He continued, "This work consists of paths, pools and terrace on the main south axis."[10]

Francis T. Underhill (1863–1929) proposed the initial change. He was born in New York and first came to Santa Barbara in the 1880s, bringing with him, according to one source, " . . . a considerable prestige in affairs social. He considered himself to be, and his intimate friends considered him to be, the arbiter in most questions of etiquette and fashion." In 1906 he married into the very prominent and affluent De la Guerra family. An outsized personality who counted architecture among his many avocations, he had worked on several local properties and is credited with designing the lower ter-

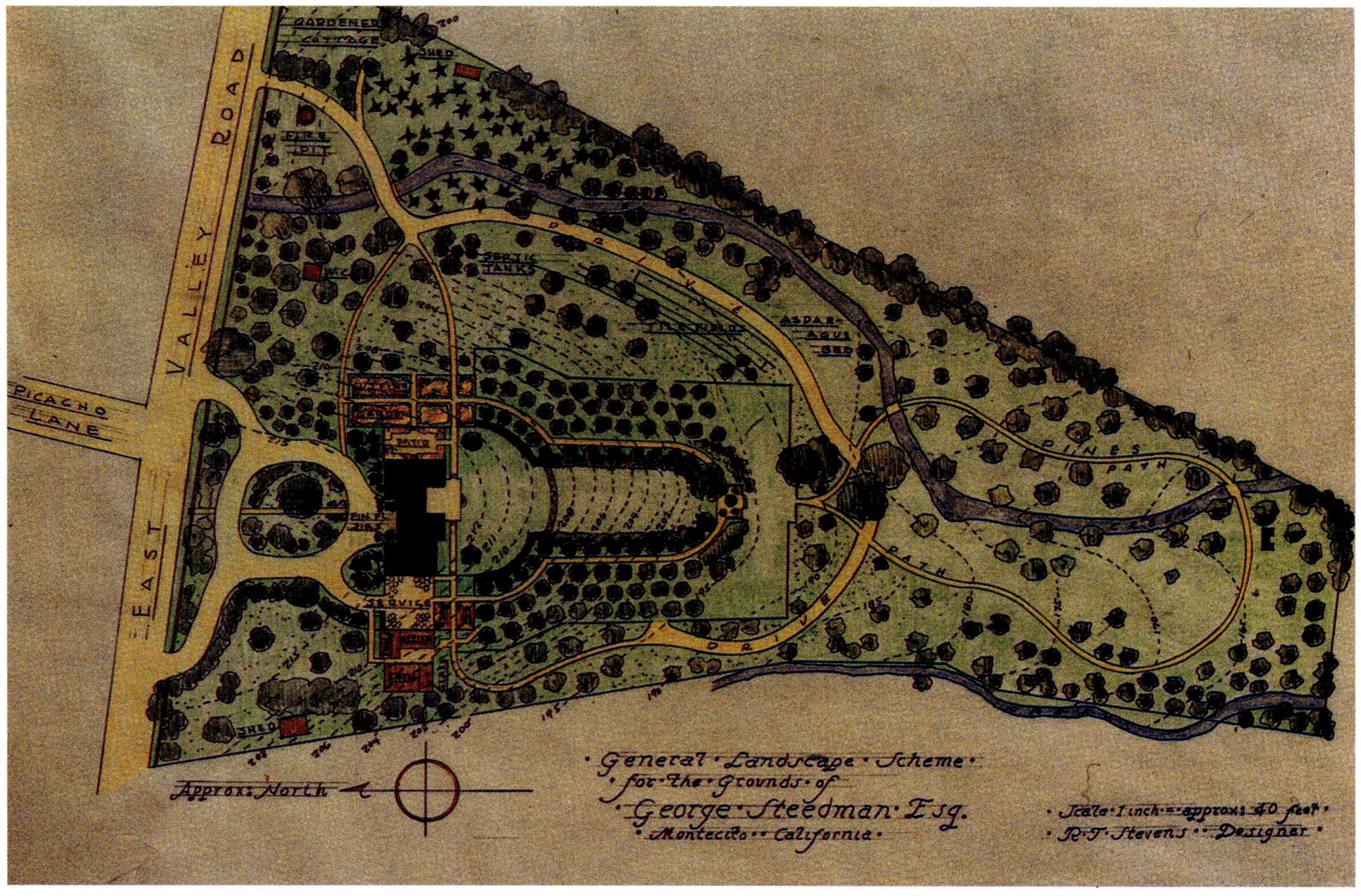

Fig. 4.4: Ralph Stevens, Casa garden plan.

race and swimming pool in the garden at Arcady, the George Owen Knapp estate. He was president of the Santa Barbara Club when Steedman stayed there in 1925; presumably they knew one another through this connection.[11]

Lockwood de Forest, Jr. (1896–1949), worked on and off at the Casa for more than a decade. Seemingly an intuitive designer, he had only minimal formal training though, according to a notice in a contemporary newspaper, he took "a course in landscape architecture" at the University of California, Berkeley, in 1919. He worked for Stevens in 1920–21 and then went to Europe for six months with a school friend, Wright Ludington. They traveled together through Italy then went their separate ways, de Forest going to Spain where he reportedly visited and photographed Moorish gardens. He returned in September 1921 and during a second stint in Stevens's office around 1923, he completed some drawings for the Casa. He then began his independent career in Santa Barbara. Between 1925 and 1942 he and his wife Elizabeth edited *Santa Barbara Gardener*, the organ of the Planting Committee of the Community Arts Association. If for no other reason his name will live in

the history of Santa Barbara gardens because of his work at Val Verde, the Ludington estate in Montecito.[12]

Underhill's work on the Casa garden is confirmed by a drawing by de Forest dated November 23, 1925. A note in de Forest's hand states:

> This scheme suggested by Mr. Underhill has been checked by him on the ground and has received his approval. Its simplicity and nice proportion meets with my unqualified approval.[13]

De Forest's drawing shows further definition of the lawn area opening from the loggia on the south front. Stevens had used curved eugenia hedges to enclose the space (see Fig. 4.4). Underhill proposed superimposing parallel brick paths bordered by low box hedge inside the eugenias, leading to paved platforms with L-shaped benches and parapets marking the transition to the lower garden (Fig. 4.6). Steedman retraced de Forest's drawing on November 29, 1925, adding his own suggestions and noting:

> I believe my changes are of detail only, and do not alter the fundamentals of Mr. Underhill—but sim-

Fig. 4.5: Casa, south garden from loggia.

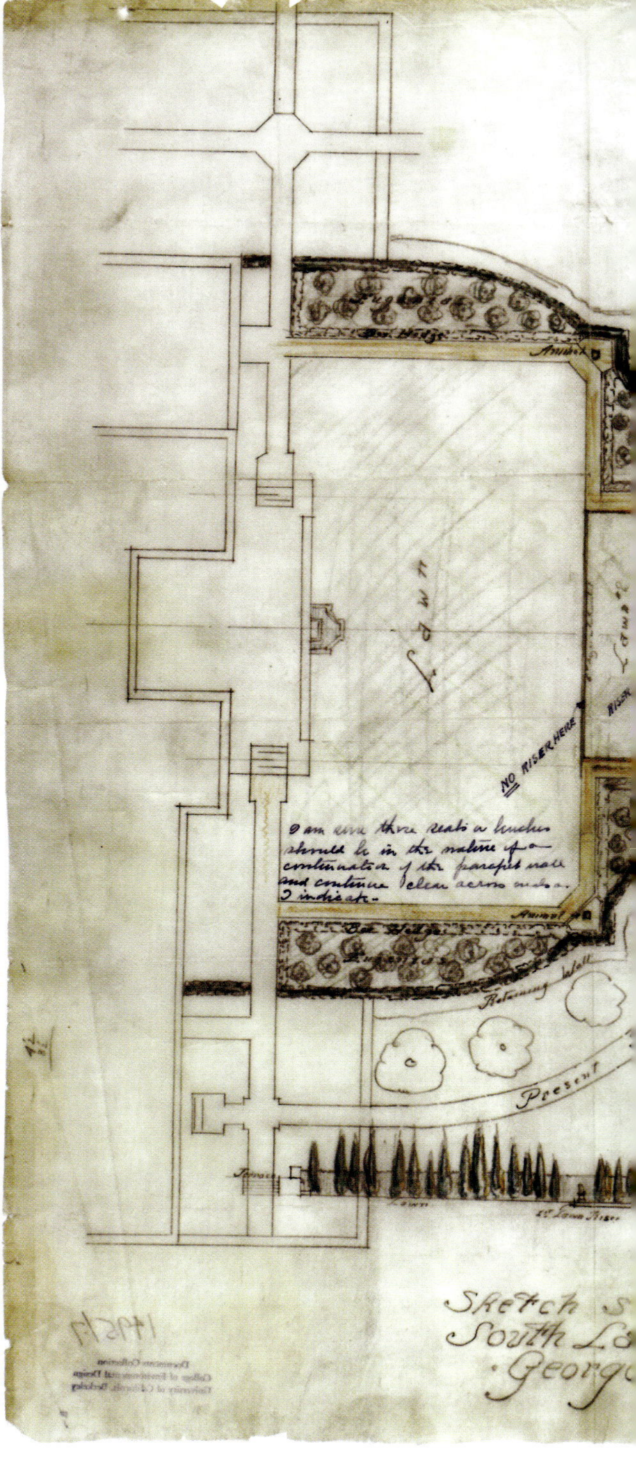

plify the details, and make the completed job more formal and in better Spanish tradition.[14]

Photographs confirm that the work was at least partially completed but had been modified by 1927. The east-west bench returns and parapet extensions leading to the lower garden were removed, possibly in conjunction with installation of the pergolas in place today (Fig. 4.5).

De Forest also established the present configuration of the north entry court at the Casa; i.e., as a rectilinear, walled and paved enclosure in contrast with the more naturalistic reminiscence carried out by Stevens. The eastern access from Valley Road was eliminated, and the court was entered axially from the north; a cross axis was created by gates leading to the service area on the west and the cutting garden on the east (Fig. 4.7). A wellhead was specified as the central focal point. Steedman made additional drawings showing the paving worked out in much greater detail and the substitution of an octagonal, tiled pool for the wellhead. One of these drawings is dated May 22, 1927, and shows the design essentially as

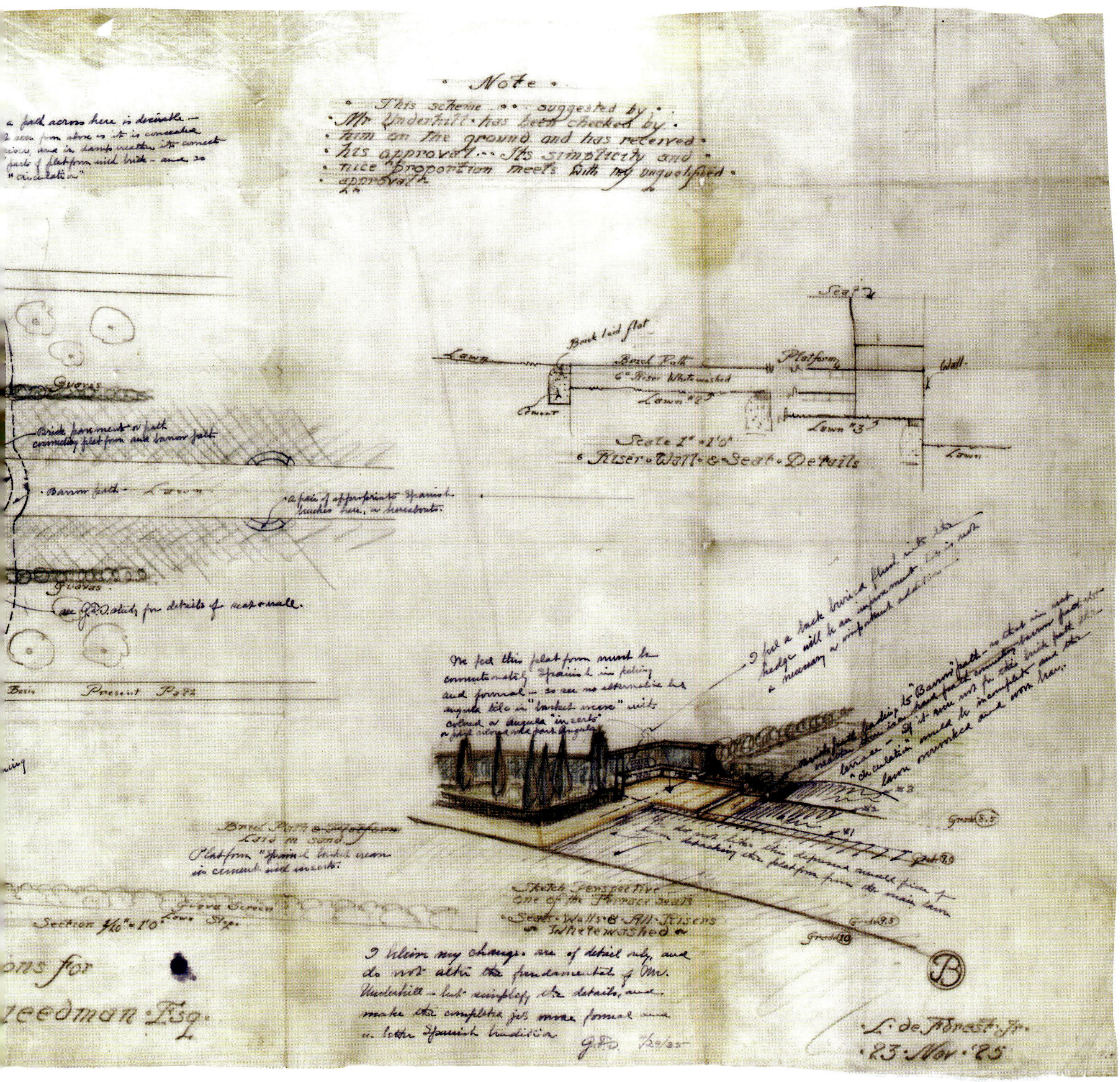

Fig. 4.6: Lockwood de Forest, Casa garden plan, November 23, 1925.

it was completed. This date coincides with the recollections of Edward Hart (1920–), who remembers his father William working with John Hartfeld on the paving. Mr. Hart explained the process:

My father, Hartfeld and another gardener gathered the pebbles on beaches between San Juan Capistrano and San Diego; several trips were necessary. A wood frame was constructed and partially filled with dry mortar mixed in a ratio of one part cement to three parts sand. The pebbles were laid in the mortar and leveled with a straight edge. Another layer of mortar was added and brushed between the pebbles and then sprayed with water, causing it to set. It was kept damp for several days.[15]

An equally important contemporary project was the installation of the star pool in the south garden; it was in place by June 1928, though there is no evidence associating this work with de Forest.[16] The pool was reworked repeatedly, both on paper and in execution; at one point Steedman installed a bowl and pedestal in the center (see Fig. 4.5). A

53

runnel leading from the fountain in the loggia parapet fed the pool; it continued to a smaller pool in the paved area laid out by Underhill and de Forest. Later the stone coping shown in early photographs was removed and replaced with tile, and a low jet producing gentle ripples on the water surface was installed.

The garden surrounding the pool was similarly reconfigured. Initially the ground was articulated into sections crisscrossed by diagonal paths, a design surely inspired by the Generalife (Fig. 4.10). In various incarnations the spaces between the paths were filled with grass, ivy, and low plants (Fig. 4.8). The octagonal concrete pads with tiled surfaces imbedded in the soil today are vestiges of the paths and originally marked points of intersection.

Clearly Steedman was experimenting. His exploration led to fussiness—though by whose hand is unclear, and not for long—which he reversed in favor of the underlying theme of simplification. His most far-reaching change, in terms both of architectural form and circulation, was the removal of the loggia parapet and fountain and replacement of them with open metal rails and cir-

cular brick steps on axis with the orientation of the garden (Fig. 4.9; see Fig. 4.8). He also simplified the immediate point of termination on the horizon. As originally constructed, the area around the "pepper tree" fountain was enclosed on three sides by a high wall; a "Moorish" doorway opened to the south, to the cactus garden and the watering trough in the distance. Steedman obviously thought the wall was an obstruction and by 1932 the southern segment had been lowered (Figs. 4.11, 5.23).

In 1927 Steedman was contemplating building a cottage for a butler or chauffeur on the northwest corner of his property and was hoping to purchase a small neighboring site to avoid grading and filling that would be required because of the sharp drop in elevation.[17] This transaction never took place and ultimately the new cottage was sited within the existing boundary lines.

Steedman turned this time not to Smith but to Edwards Plunkett & Howell, another Santa Barbara firm working in the Spanish Colonial idiom, to design the cottage. William Albert Edwards (1888–1976) had been practicing in Santa Barbara

Fig. 4.8 Casa,
south elevation.

Fig. 4.9 Casa,
south elevation.

since 1919; after the 1925 earthquake he formed a partnership with Joseph Plunkett (1900–1946). Henry Howell (1889–1962) joined the firm in 1926 but left after two years. Although Edwards & Plunkett went on to design the Fox Arlington Theater—one of the great monuments of Spanish Colonial Revival architecture—and the Santa Barbara airport, in the late twenties their portfolio consisted of small commercial buildings and a few houses.[18]

Steedman and Edwards, Plunkett & Howell signed a contract for the butler's cottage, May 3, 1928; the plans and specifications were delivered in October. Howell, explaining the delay to Steedman, noted a familiar pattern: "The changes and revisions which were made necessitated re-drawing the plans several times, and we were anxious to have the building planned exactly as you wished as well as a credit to us architecturally, which we are sure it will be."[19]

The new cottage had three bedrooms and must have been designed with the first butler, William G. Hart (1883–1974), his wife and two sons, in mind. It was two stories but was visible as such only from the rear or south elevation because of the steep grade. Stylistically it conforms to the Andalusian farmhouse mode and was built between October 1928 and January 1929 (Fig. 4.12).

Fig. 4.10: Casa, south garden.

Fig. 4.11: Casa, pepper tree fountain and Moorish gate.

Fig. 4.12: Edwards,
Plunkett & Howell,
butler's cottage.

Fig. 4.13: Edwards
& Plunkett, well
house.

Edwards & Plunkett also designed a new well house to replace the water tower that was built in 1922. Still standing on Picacho Lane, across Valley Road from the Casa, it is a simple structure comprising an equipment room and reservoir (Fig. 4.13). Spanish allusions and decorative tile embellishment belie its pragmatic function. The structure was completed in 1929 and received an honorable mention award as "Among the Best Examples of Civic and Commercial Architecture Erected in Santa Barbara . . . . " that year by the Community Arts Association Plans and Planting Branch. Steedman responded to Pearl Chase, "I did the engineering planning only – Plunkett did the architectural work without any suggestion from me so I feel any credit is due his firm for the architectural quality . . . ."[21]

ceramic tiles. Steedman purchased a limited quantity in Spain in 1923, far less than he needed. Two groups, seven hundred three-inch-square tiles from the reign of Charles V (1516–56), used in the entrance and stair hall floors, and eleven Alcora tiles, were "antique." The rest were generally "second hand," probably "less than 100 years old."[23] The initial order from Chemla in 1924 was for 7,220 tiles for which Byne had specific allocations in mind: the main stair, the beauty parlor and bathrooms.[24]

In a distinct change in sensibilities—in 1923 Steedman stated that he wanted "<u>very</u> <u>little</u> tile"—he soon developed an almost insatiable desire for it.[25] He placed a second order with Chemla for approximately five thousand tiles in March 1925 and though this order had not been shipped by June 1927 Steedman

According to Joe Acquistapace, Steedman's gardener, there were functional problems almost immediately:

> The well he engineered, the second year that I was there that well wasn't producing enough water, so he sunk a new one right alongside of it, 450' deep. But it's all Curtis Manufacturing machinery in there, the centrifugal pumps and what have you. It's pumped by air—from the top air goes down one pipe to 400 and some odd feet, not quite to the bottom, and it comes up and pushes the water out of another one.[22]

Threaded throughout the construction and furnishing of the Casa is a minor saga about decorative

contacted Chemla again, expressing interest in purchasing an additional 5,200 units. He continued, "I admire and like your tile very much, but it is distressing that you will not answer letters. . . . Won't you please be perfectly frank and tell me whether you are going to ship and whether you want orders?"[26] A year later Steedman wrote to Byne, "I take it for granted that the dear, damn Chemla has not as yet started on this order. . . ."[27]

The orders finally arrived in Santa Barbara in early 1929. Steedman installed the tile over the next three years, embellishing both the house and garden. The display of tile at the Casa is astonishing, perhaps nowhere more so than in the beauty parlor,

Steedman's bedroom and the garage. Old Spanish and modern Tunisian tiles are combined freely. In the beauty parlor large and small Alcora and Catalan figure tiles are juxtaposed with no fewer than nine patterns from Chemla (Figs. 4.14, 4.15). The fireplace in Steedman's bedroom is composed primarily of sixteenth-century tiles from a convent in Segovia that display interlocking circular and square patterns—the same tiles that figure prominently in the octagonal pool in the front courtyard and the pergola benches in the south garden—combined with Alcora figure tiles and Chemla borders (see Fig. 3.13).

One might be tempted to conclude that Steedman went overboard in the garage but there was a rationale. In June 1928 he explained that the floor was paved with ten-inch red square tiles and that because of oil dripping from the cars it was "impossible to keep the floor in a presentable condition." He proposed installing " . . . what might be termed a tile rug in the floors under the automobiles." He wanted to lay "negro black" tiles in two rectangular areas about five by fourteen feet each with con-

trasting tile borders. At the same time he wanted to add a tile dado because the ground level outside the garage was about sixteen inches higher than the floor " . . . and I cannot keep any paint on the wall."[28] The combined effect of the tiles, the fine stone arch and the hunting trophies mounted on the walls is as eye-catching as the Packards Steedman kept there (Fig. 4.16).

Steedman continued to initiate projects large and small through the mid-1930s; ongoing construction became a way of life at the Casa. In December 1930 Lutah Maria Riggs prepared plans for reconfiguring the service areas of the house, expanding the space into the southern garage and modifying the circulation. As the house was constructed, parallel circulation routes led from the entrance hall to the dining room and stair hall, and to the service areas and garages beyond. The two paths were replaced with one, the doorways from the entrance hall to the dining room and on through to the pantry and kitchen being plastered over. At the same time, a new safe for

silver and a closet were placed in the original garage space, and a stair to the servant bedrooms was added. A porch was incorporated into the adjoining servants' dining room and a new door at the end of the hall opened to the service court. A "flower bench" was placed in the former garage opening on the west facade (Fig. 4.17). The work was completed in March and April 1931. Presumably at the same time a wall dividing the dining room and stair hall was removed (Fig. 4.18).

The butler's cottage was expanded several times; work began in 1929 with the addition of a two-room apartment for a chauffeur (today the offices of Casa del Herrero Foundation) designed by Steedman. In 1931 two garages designed by Riggs were added. As first completed, the cottage had two garages at the southeastern corner of the building with a gabled roof oriented perpendicularly to the gable of the main house. The new garages were added to the north and the four covered by a roof with a ridge parallel with the house. Typically, the construction process was complicated. Riggs noted, " . . . Kenyon has just advised me that the revised estimate which he planned to get from his subcontractors for you, is absolutely impossible because of the numerous changes and discoveries which have unavoidably occurred every day since the beginning of construction."[29]

In early 1933 Riggs prepared drawings for a second story addition to the shop, in essence a living room, bedroom and bath for a servant. The only evidence suggesting that this was constructed is a photograph showing two chimneys corresponding to fireplaces on the plan that otherwise cannot be reconciled with the shop itself (Fig. 4.19). In any case the entire building was demolished a year later.

Fig. 4.19: Garage
court.

Fig. 4.20: Lutah
Maria Riggs, book
tower at left.

Riggs followed up in 1933 with a minor tour de force, a "book tower" addition projecting diagonally from the living room and linked to it by a gently curved passage. Its steel framing belies its medieval inspiration (Fig. 4.20). Octagonal in plan and just over half the height of the main building, it has the diminutive quality of a playhouse. The interior, with its gilded trim, is Gothic in spirit, a quality enhanced by the frieze of panels inspired by *Speculum Humanae, Salvation's Block Book*, circa 1470, hand-painted by Channing Peake (Figs. 4.21, 4.22, 4.24).[30] The sacristy door Steedman purchased in Paris in 1924 was moved here from the living room where it had previously covered a wall cabinet (Fig. 4.23).

The final major construction at Casa del Herrero was a new shop to replace the first one completed in 1925 and possibly enlarged in 1933 by Riggs. Floyd Brewster, who was working in Smith's office during construction of the Casa, designed the new building. He had been devastated by the Depression, and in October 1933, while the book tower was under construction, wrote to Steedman urgently requesting a $400 loan. He explained that his income in the last two years had been $400 and that he was about to lose his house on Mission Canyon Road. Steedman responded affirmatively and offered temporary work in his shop if necessary. He noted later, "Brewster worked on drawings from 3/3/34 to 6/8/34 and worked out $400 @ 15¢ hour–" (a mathematical impossibility).[31] These drawings led to the new workshop.

Fig. 4.21: Lutah Maria Riggs, book tower.

Fig. 4.22: Book tower detail.

Fig. 4.23: Carved sacristy door.

FOLLOWING PAGES
Fig. 4.24: Book tower ceiling with Mexican silver chandelier and frieze panels painted by Channing Peake.

Tribulation of Job
The prodigal returns
Whale swallows Jonah
Christ leaves hell
Whale casts up Jonah

Expulsion · from · eden + Adam · delved · eve · span + Noah · builds · me · ark ·
· love · + · Angel · reprimands · Baalam · ·
Return of the dove +
nis · bloc · b · or · c · 1470

Brewster is architect of record but there can be no doubt that the building is less an artistic endeavor on his part than a pragmatic response to Steedman's needs.

The original shop was located west of the Casa across a stone-paved garage court. It could be entered from the court and also from the garden below. The new building was constructed on the same site but was two stories high and roughly three times the size. Because of the drop in grade, it appears to be only one story high from the court (Figs. 4.25–4.28). Possibly to reduce the visual bulk, the elevation facing the court was reduced twelve feet in length on the south end (the original shop extended the length of the courtyard wall); the building instead was extended to the west. The shop itself was on the upper level and included an office for Steedman that incorporated the leaded windows removed from the dining room in 1925. Rooms for producing and storing wine were below. Construction continued from May to November 1934 at a cost of $22,000. Bantering, Steedman's brother Edwin commented, "It is perfectly apparent that you should employ me on an annual retainer to act as your guardian. For example, my advice was sound to have you build a new shop and wine cellar, but I did not expect you to have it inlaid with mosaics and probably bronze centaurs for decorations; otherwise I don't see how you could spend the 20 grand."[32]

Three garden buildings: a greenhouse and potting and tool sheds completed the construction

projects at the Casa. They were placed immediately to the west of the workshop and probably completed in late 1934; Steedman signed the drawings.

Arthur Byne and Mildred Stapley, in their book *Provincial Houses in Spain*, 1925, focus largely on *cortijos*: Andalusian farmhouses and their surrounding service units. These groups of buildings were often on an enormous scale analogous to a small town and were completely walled in. Because of inaccessibility resulting from great distances aggravated by nearly impassable roads, they were largely self-sufficient and serviced by large staffs. They often included shops and forgeries and cellars for making wine though living quarters for the master may or may not have been provided. Usually the buildings were strictly utilitarian architecturally and structurally, though in some instances there were "certain indulgences" including colored tiles and *rejas*.[33]

The spirit of the *cortijo* if not the reality pervades Casa del Herrero Estate. In addition to the productive activities of metalworking and winemaking, there was at least the semblance of self-sufficiency in the orchards and kitchen garden. And at its peak in the early 1930s with maids; a butler, cook, chauffeur, and laundress; staff members' children and more than a dozen gardeners on hand at any given time, the estate was nothing less than a small fiefdom for the Steedmans.

Fig. 4.26: (above left top): George Washington Smith, service court.

Fig. 4.27: (bottom left): Floyd E. Brewster, shop, 1934.

Fig. 4.28: (above) George Washington Smith, service court.

CHAPTER 5

Life in the Casa

*As usual, I am just as busy as a bird dog in a briar patch, doing nothing. I never was
any busier when I was doing real, honest work. I didn't know an old horse could have
so much fun on pasture, with half a leg left to stand on, as I enjoy out here.*[1]

Casa del Herrero Estate with its ten-and-a-half-acre site and seven-thousand-square-foot house was comparatively modest by Montecito standards. It was conceived as a winter house for a couple barely middle-aged—George was 54; Carrie was 50—when they first moved in. Their older daughter Katherine was 20 and seldom in residence; Medora, the younger, was 15 and did spend time there.[2] Large-scale entertaining was not anticipated, as Steedman explained in 1924: "We very seldom sit down more than eight to a meal . . . . "[3] Nor was there accommodation for many overnight visitors. Initial provision for staffing was conservative: there were three servant bedrooms in the Casa in addition to the separate gardener's cottage.

Though the Steedmans were in residence at the Casa only intermittently between 1925 and 1930, they quickly assimilated with local gentry. They were greeted shortly after they moved in by the prominent local artist DeWitt Parshall and his wife—who had their own George Washington Smith house—at a dinner at Edgecliffe.[4] In addition to the Santa Barbara Club, they joined the Montecito Country Club in 1923, and in 1928 became charter members of the Valley Club. Steedman also listed the La Cumbre Country Club in his Harvard class report of 1928 and the 1931 *Blue Book of Santa Barbara* mentions membership in the Little Town Club.[5] Max Fleischmann and Dwight Murphy, the most powerful and public-spirited activists in Santa Barbara, were in their orbit.

Writing to the Santa Barbara *Morning Press* in 1936, Steedman commented that he had always kept his name out of the papers and hated publicity, though from time to time—as in St. Louis—both his and Carrie's activities were noted. In April 1928 the Santa Barbara and Los Angeles papers reported a dinner they attended in honor of Charles Lindbergh, who was still the subject of national adulation because of his 1927 flight from New York to Paris. Harry F. Guggenheim, President of the Daniel Guggenheim Fund for the Promotion of Aeronautics in New York, and his wife gave the dinner in their cottage at the new Santa Barbara Biltmore Hotel. Guggenheim met Lindbergh before the flight and subsequently sponsored a cross-country tour for the pilot from July to October 1927. Other guests at the dinner included supporters from St. Louis who had gone to Santa Barbara with Lindbergh: Harry Hall Knight, President of the St. Louis Flying Club; Harold M. Bixby, President of the St. Louis Chamber of Commerce; Major William B. Robertson, President of the Robertson Aircraft Company for whom Lindbergh had been flying as a mail pilot; and Dwight Murphy.[6]

The Steedmans' involvement in Santa Barbara civic affairs was limited but they were generous in opening their garden to the public on a regular basis. Garden tours began in Santa Barbara in 1925 and have been a way of life ever since.[7] The embryonic Casa garden was first shown on the occasion of the Thirteenth Annual Meeting of the Garden Club of America held in Santa Barbara in April 1926. Ninety-nine club members departed from Grand Central Station in New York and made their way west on a thirteen-car New York Central "Garden Club of America Special." The group stopped first in Pasadena and then traveled on to Santa Barbara where they remained for four days, using El Mirasol, a luxury cottage hotel on Micheltorena Street across from Alameda Park, as their headquarters. Casa del Herrero was on the first day's program; the *Garden Club Bulletin* described it as a:

. . . perfect Spanish house. From iron-railed balconies over the front door a superb piece of old Spanish brocade was hung; candle-lanterns with cut glass shields were clamped to the rails. The floors of the hall are of waxed tile, the decorated ceilings are Spanish 16th Century. The paneling was brought from Spain and the hand tooled or decorated bolts, doors and tiles came from Tunis and Algiers. There was an interesting cactus planting in the court-yard, some, very low growing, with yuccas and Century plants, etc. A little garden at one end of the house is a copy of the Gereriliffe [*sic*]; below it, down two steps, is a cutting garden and we were immensely interested in Mrs. Steedman's demonstration of planting from tin cans. In California plants can be bought by the gallon—that is, they are grown in tin cans of one, two, three, four or five gallons and delivered with the can attached. The cans are cut down each side to the bottom with heavy metal shears, the plants slipped into their permanent position and the deed is done. It is a neat and quick method, and universally in use. Beyond a grove of Monterey pines was an herb garden, over the wall tall cactus looked from the other side. This garden was extremely interesting.[8]

If the description suggests that the house made a stronger impression than the garden, it is nonetheless interesting for its mention of cactus in the courtyard and the apparent novelty of purchasing plants in tin cans.

The Garden Club of Santa Barbara and Montecito California was established in 1916. It was a significant social outlet early on; contemporary membership lists read like a roster of the owners of the grandest Montecito houses. Unsurprisingly there was political affiliation as well. The minutes of the 1929 annual meeting note that the club "has co-operated with the Plans and Planting Committee (the provenance of Pearl Chase, one of the primary forces behind the reconstruction of Santa Barbara in the Spanish style after the 1925 earthquake) in much of its work, contributing largely towards the making of the extremely popular 'Garden Tours' an entire success . . . . "[9]

Carrie Steedman joined the local garden club in 1926 and served as president for two years, 1932–34. She made the Casa available for meetings and worked on various committees before and after her term in office. In 1932 she contributed shrubs to a project of eighth-grade students at the Orcutt School who had started a bird refuge and in 1935 the *Los Angeles Times* published a photograph of her awarding a medal for wildlife conservation in her role as chairman of the club's conservation committee.[10]

The Steedmans' lifestyle in Montecito was conditioned partly by his health, as he reported to the *Harvard College Class of 1892 Report* in 1928:

> My heart is not in good shape, and I am out of all active business or social affairs . . . and live a very quiet and uneventful life, spending my winters here (Santa Barbara, California) . . . . Of course I miss the active life, but I find great pleasure in books and such sedentary pursuits as practicing gothic painting, silversmithing, and collecting old books on these subjects, and on architecture—and I feel very lucky that Harvard gave me a liking for such things. I also feel lucky in being able to live in this beautiful country and wonderful climate, so my lot is a happy one even if I am handicapped. I advise all '92 men to look forward to a sojourn in Santa Barbara so as to get used to a heavenly existence.[11]

His statement aside, Steedman had not withdrawn entirely from business activity. In 1927 he pursued an interest in subdividing and developing tracts of land in Montecito. He discussed the idea with James R. H. Wagner, a real estate agent, who advised strongly against the proposal, describing conditions that were telling then and seem extraordinary today:

> I have gone into the matter, which we discussed, quite thoroughly. I regret to say that my analysis of the situation tells me that there is nothing attractive in purchasing the available land . . . .

Fig. 5.2: Map of Montecito.

. . . the past twenty years has [*sic*] never shown a Montecito subdivision being rapidly sold . . . .

The Spaulding Tract, at San Ysidro Road and the Coast Highway, also the Ivydean [*sic*: Ivydene] Tract, bounded by San Leandro Lane on the south and east and the San Ysidro Road on the west, are marked examples of failures as subdivisions . . . . The "San Ysidro Estates" . . . is another example.

The Hall Subdivision on the Coast Highway to the east of Miramar, has been a tragic failure . . . .

The strange anomaly is that Montecito is conceded to be one of the most beautiful residential districts in California, but the actual transfer of property, and this refers to small parcels, as well as large, are [*sic*] exceedingly few.

After all I have said, which sound [*sic*] most discouraging, I must acknowledge that there has not been a subdivision put on the market, in Montecito, which according to the rules of a good subdivider has been handled intelligently.[12]

Steedman was not dissuaded. A month later he and Wagner entered into a trust agreement in which Steedman would fund acquisition of property in the spirit of "protecting" and "improving" the neighborhood and "possibly making a profit." For the purposes of the agreement, "neighborhood" referred to "all . . . property immediately contiguous to" the Casa, and particularly abutting East Valley, Hot Springs, School House, and San Ysidro Roads. Wagner was to handle all details and receive a commission on any sales.[13]

Steedman purchased five tracts. Two, the contiguous Conrad and Contarini parcels were immediately across East Valley Road from the Casa. The Knolls land abutted the eastern boundary of the Casa. Langley Hill was south of East Valley and east of San Ysidro Roads and Parker was in Spanish Town, the area southwest of the intersection of East Valley and Hot Springs Avenue and immediately across from the house on Hot Springs Steedman had rented in 1922 (Fig. 5.2).

The Conrad tract was of greatest interest. Steedman had built a water tower there in 1922 and paid Lyde V. Conrad a regular fee for access to the water. The strategy in 1927 was to sell the bulk of the property, keeping the well site and getting water basically without cost; the deed for this thirty-three-by-fifty-foot plot was recorded in 1930.[14]

Steedman's decision to purchase the five tracts seems a rare miscalculation on his part. The Langley Hill tract was the only one on which he received any immediate return. The subdivided lots were extremely modest with fifty-foot frontages; to entice buyers, Steedman and Wagner purchased three "second-hand" houses and re-erected them on the site. By June 1928 sixteen of the forty-eight lots had been sold. But this success was offset by

the failure of other properties to sell; by recurrent sewage issues; by the need to maintain existing substandard houses that had been rented and, during the Depression, by renters falling into arrears.[15] By 1932 none of the lots in the Knowles tract east of the Casa had been sold.

The Steedmans moved to Santa Barbara permanently in 1930. The next year they participated in the annual Santa Barbara National Horse Show. Founded in 1919, the show had been derailed by the 1925 earthquake. Only in 1931 through the efforts of Dwight Murphy, Max Fleischmann and County Supervisor Sam Stanwood was it resumed. Steedman responded to Stanwood's overture for support: "I am not a horse enthusiast – but in order to participate in the constructive activities of your beautiful city I am glad to become one of the underwriters of your horse show enterprise to the extent of five hundred dollars a year for three years."[16]

Steedman's contribution must have led to his wife's seemingly surprising entry in the racing competition. According to the Santa Barbara and Los Angeles papers, "Pink Boy [*sic*: Pinky] exhibited by Mrs. George F. Steedman and ridden by John Van Dusen, [placed] third . . . ."[17]

The papers also noted Carrie Steedman's election to the board of trustees of the Santa Barbara Museum of Natural History in 1934, the same time that Max Fleischmann became president. This was the only museum in Santa Barbara (the art museum opened in the vacated post office building on State Street in 1941) and it served for several years as a venue for Garden Club activities, surely her interest in serving.[18]

While Carrie was to some extent reaching out into the community, George was retreating, as he indicated once again in the *Harvard College Class of 1932 Report*:

I have not done an honest day's work since Armistice Day, 1918.

I am afflicted (or blessed?) with an incurable heart disease, which, if I take life easy, will probably permit me to live to a ripe and happy old age, and I am enjoying a regular and easy life in southern California. Shooting, golf, and all exercise are no longer permitted, but my life work of engi-

Fig. 5.3: George Steedman working in the original shop, 1931.

neering, machinery, and the like gave me a training that now permits me to spend many happy hours each day as a sedentary silversmith—a vegetable existence perhaps, but a very happy and contented life on pasture, after plenty of hard work and activity in my younger days.

My two daughters are married, and Mrs. Steedman and I live nearly all year in our home in Santa Barbara. I recommend Santa Barbara to all Harvard '92 as as near a Heaven as you can find on earth.[19]

For George Steedman, the shop was the holy land at Casa del Herrero Estate; he was photographed working in the original building in 1931 (Fig. 5.3). It was equipped primarily for multi-disciplined metalworking though there also were woodworking tools and an area set aside for flower arranging.

Steedman's chief artistic avocation was silversmithing. He explained to Paul Dudley White in 1936:

I have found really great happiness in attempting to turn out a grade of work which compares with the old English and Irish silver work of from two to three hundred years ago. It serves a temporary [therapeutic] cause, and I also feel it is a permanent thing, which will live long after I am gone.[20]

His interest can be traced to the mid-1920s when he wrote to Goldsmith Brothers Smelting & Refining Company in Chicago inquiring about availability and prices for silver sheets and bars which he might use to make forks and spoons by what he called the "hand hammer" process. Tongue-in-cheek, he also inquired about the firm's policy on repurchasing scrap silver as he expected to produce nothing but scrap for a considerable time. He followed up in 1927, taking nine lessons in Boston from George Gebelein, perhaps America's foremost silversmith of the twentieth century.[21]

Simply stated, sterling silver is an alloy of silver, copper, tin and antimony that can be cast, forged, raised (hammered), hollowed, seamed, and creased into desired shapes. Sheet silver can be spun on a lathe to create round, hollow metal forms in an infinite variety of profiles such as dishes or bowls. Silver objects can be decorated with repoussé (a process of forming relief patterns by hammering on the back side) and chased (a similar process done on the front side). Steedman employed all of these techniques in his silver work (Figs. 5.4–5.6).

The furnace in the northwest corner of the shop served for casting objects in the age-old lost wax process. First, the desired object is carved by hand in wax. The model is then encased in a heat-resistant material, the wax is melted and drained off and molten metal is poured into the resultant cavity. After cooling, the protective material is broken away, leaving the desired object. Steedman repro-duced bronze lion finials purchased in Barcelona in this manner (Figs. 5.7–5.9).

The brazing and annealing station, which shows in photographs of the first shop, would have been used to solder pieces of silver together and to heat and soften silver that had become brittle from hammering. It is equipped with a turntable and a small furnace and gas torches to heat pieces to appropriate temperatures. The shop also has an anvil and hammers for blacksmithing—more ancient technology—and modern power saws and sanders for working with wood, though examples of woodworking are few in comparison to metal. Steedman designed the adjustable "reclining couch" now in the sleeping porch and presumably produced it in the shop; his drawing is signed and dated January 1930. Assembled with both old and new materials, it brings to mind the nineteenth-century mechanical furniture for which numerous patents were issued (Fig. 5.10). The sundial with

Fig. 5.10: George Steedman, reclining couch, 1930.

FACING PAGE
Fig. 5.11: George Steedman, sundial, 1930.

its whimsical homilies in the south garden is another of Steedman's shop designs from the same period (Fig. 5.11).[22]

The shop is a tribute to Steedman's inventiveness, safety concerns and sense of organization. There are pivoting overhead lights constructed of curved pipe and tin cans, an ingenious ceiling-mounted pulley system to operate a lathe, and a counterbalanced cable for opening the door to the furnace. Blade guards for saws are labeled "remove at your own risk." Drawers, shelves and bins are fastidiously labeled to keep each tool or supply in its place; soiled rags are distinguished from flammable rags (Figs. 5.12–5.15).

Fig. 5.12: Detail of shop, 1934.

The lower floor of the shop building contains rooms for making wine, an activity at Casa del Herrero that dates from the late twenties (Figs. 5.16, 5.17). In 1929 John Hartfeld produced Zinfandel from grapes purchased locally; Steedman commented that it was "... very thick, fatty and sweet." Steedman took detailed notes on each year's output, describing both the process and, at least in the early years, the uneven results. Never shy about asking for advice, in 1931, after noting that "many errors were made," he wrote to Paul Masson, the well-known winemaker in San Jose, inquiring about purchasing small quantities of grapes. Masson agreed and offered the observation that "Making grape juice is more simple than most people think" and that Steedman's mistake was to "... try to urge nature by filtering through a screen or cheesecloth;" and that the "... containers must be clean, full and airtight and then trust nature." The next year, Masson stated, "Practically . . . there is [*sic*] no good wine grapes grown outside of . . . Sonoma, Napa and Santa Clara Counties," an opinion that has not survived the test of time.[23]

Steedman produced wine virtually until his death, purchasing his grapes from Masson and other vineyards. Although his "little winery" was "... nothing but a toy laboratory" and was by his own admission an expensive means to an end, it provided an opportunity to produce unique wines that could not be purchased commercially. And his results improved. In the past he made "... a good many mistakes . . . " and "... had to throw away quite a considerable percentage of the wine I have made." By 1936 he told Masson that he was "... greatly pleased with the results of my last two or three years of wine making. I have learned to use your grapes and am making much better wine than I ever expected to be able to make as an amateur."[24]

Steedman routinely invited apprentices to work with him in the shop. His interest can be traced to a proposal he submitted to the school of architecture at Harvard in 1928 in which he offered to establish an endowment of $200,000, the income from which was to be used for "... the education and craft training of young men and/or young women in Architecture . . . or any other practical art or craft allied to Architecture." He expressed the hope that administration of the fund would "... be put in the hands of those who are in sympathy with the idea of combining . . . the advantages of an old-fashioned apprenticeship with a modern University education."[25]

Two of the shop apprentices, Channing Peake and Gordon Grant, are remembered today. Peake (1910–1989) attended the California School of Arts and Crafts in Oakland in the late 1920s where he met fellow student Campbell Grant, younger brother of Gordon. The two became friends and in 1929 they transferred to the Santa Barbara School of the Arts.[26]

Fig. 5.14: Detail of shop, 1934.

Fig. 5.15: Floyd E. Brewster, the shop, 1934.

BURNABLE RUBBISH
SOILED · RAGS ·
FINISH
BOX

Fig. 5.13: Detail of shop, 1934.

Figs. 5.16, 5.17 (facing page): Shop/wine cellar, 1934.

88076-11131
San Mi
BURG
DON MIGUEL

Peake worked with Steedman for approximately a year in 1933–34; Casa records indicate that he was paid as a draftsman. Late in life he recalled the experience in an interview with Cynthia Haskell:

PEAKE : "Then I was hired by a man in Montecito named George Steedman which gave me a job. I was hired to . . . work in the . . . . He was a silversmith, a retired wealthy man from St. Louis and he needed somebody to translate Gothic designs that he liked very much so that he could work in silver in them. That was an interesting experience in many ways. I mean it was really . . . a great education.

He . . . was a Harvard man with all the background and he had a fantastic collection of books, which . . . I spent a good deal of time with because . . . they were open to me. And he treated me at first as an apprentice and he treated himself as a Medici. So it wasn't hard to take . . . . He was a difficult person, he hated to show any affection and it was maybe . . . a year and a half before he really opened up. His wife was a marvelous lady who was gone to the woman's club most of the time and so . . . he didn't have anybody, he had these marvelous meals . . . and he had the silver and the goblets and the whole thing but he didn't have any company.

82

HASKELL: Sounds a little lonely.

PEAKE: Yeah. So finally he broke down, not in any official sense, but he invited me in to have lunch with him. So I dropped the paper bag deal and it started that way and he was also doing a little wine research on his own. And this was not . . . prohibition but you weren't supposed to make your own wine and with . . . these lovely silver goblets and tasting these various wines after lunch . . . he'd go up for his siesta and I'd go back to the shop where we worked and try to stay awake. Well anyway . . . it had reality and it didn't.

HASKELL : Sounds like a dilemma.

PEAKE : Oh I could have been, you know, in the Renaissance, that part of my life.[27]

Peake's tenure was brief but he left his mark. He didn't say so in the interview, but he is credited with painting the frieze in the book tower. He also painted panels in the beauty parlor ceiling and probably the fireplace hood in the dining room and the niche in the living room now housing phonograph equipment (Fig. 5.18).

Gordon Kenneth Grant (1908–1940) worked in the Casa shop between 1935 and 1940; surely his brother's friendship with Channing Peake led to the introduction to Steedman. Something of his relationship with Steedman comes from Steedman's notes: "no specified hours-no arrangement as to period of employment–I told him he could quit when he wished."[28]

Seemingly Grant's first undertaking was to revisit designs for metal chairs for the loggia and other outdoor areas that Steedman had worked out in 1932 but did not build at the time. Given the monikers "Senora Herrero" and "Don Herrero," the chairs were to be fabricated with frames of Duralumin (du-RAL-u-min), an aluminum alloy containing copper, manganese and magnesium that was relatively soft and could be worked in a variety of shapes; it was favored by the aircraft industry in the early 1930s because of its lightness and strength (Figs. 5.19, 5.20).[29] Sheet aluminum or copper incised with a diaper pattern to suggest leather was specified for the seats and backs. The chairs were to be assembled with Duralumin rivets, bolts, nuts and washers.

Grant did not tamper with Steedman's basic premise of expressing medieval aesthetics with twentieth-century technology. He did substitute a decorative heraldic shield with anvil and trowels for a flower motif Steedman had proposed for the center of the back of the "Senora Herrero" chair (Figs. 5.21, 5.22). Several of each chair—*Senora* and *Don*—and a smaller version without arms were probably fabricated in 1936. Grant's device appears on all but one.

Steedman also built several low stools or *banquettes* that are ingenious in the manner in which he replicated the S-shaped saw-cut in the seats of the wooden prototypes inside the Casa. Because the sheet metal was thin, he added a block or boss on the underside for reinforcement.

Grant's unstructured relationship with Steedman gave him license to pursue outside interests; a contemporary article in the Santa Barbara *Morning Press* indicates that he maintained a studio at 826 Garden Street.[30] Grant was deeply influenced by

Figs. 5.19–5.22: Metal furniture

Fig. 5.23: *Staff lunch, December 24, 1932. A note in Steedman's hand on the verso includes the menu and then continues: "5 regular men and 5 extras-extras were of the 'unemployed' they were laid off after lunch as all work was finished-"*

Native American Indian culture and much of his work was informed by travel in the Southwest. Edward Alden Jewell, art critic for the *New York Times*, praised Grant in a 1935 review of work submitted in competition for the Prix de Rome fellowship: "There are some highly effective formalized designs based on the art of the American Indian by Gordon K. Grant . . . . " Three years later the *Los Angeles Times* art critic Arthur Millier noted, "Eagle Dance at Santa Clara,' a panel by Gordon Kenneth Grant . . . took top spot prize . . . ", also in competition. He continued, "The same artist shows a more impressive, bigger 'Buffalo Dance.' Both are novel, spirited but only surface deep."[31]

Grant's most visible accomplishment—completed while he was under Steedman's wing—resulted from his participation in a Depression era program of government-sponsored public art. The initiative began in 1933 as the Public Works of Art Project and was extended and redefined several times. Between 1938 and 1943 the program was called the Section of Fine Arts whose mission was to place murals in new post offices. The subject matter was to be accessible to as many people as possible and to " . . . follow the American Scene style associated with Thomas Hart Benton and others who had been inspired by Diego Rivera and other Mexican muralists." Grant completed several murals under this program. His ability to adapt to

bureaucratic standards is displayed in two that survive, in the Ventura, California (1938), and Brady, Texas (1939) post offices.[32]

Initially the Casa seems to have been minimally staffed. In addition to John Hartfeld, William Hart was on hand to work on various special projects, notably the paving of the entry court; he also served as butler when the Steedmans were in residence. He and his family became the first occupants of the butler's cottage when it was completed in 1929; they remained until mid-1931. The staff increased significantly when the Steedmans became full-time residents in 1930; they settled into a lifestyle of quiet formality. Over the years there were variously a butler and cook, two or three maids, a chauffeur and a full-time gardener living in the Casa and in the two other houses on the property. Edward H. Hart, Hart's younger son, recalled in 2005 that even meals taken alone were served ceremoniously by his father and that each meal required proper attire.[33] In addition to the full-time staff in residence, numerous day laborers were on hand to work on Steedman's special projects and to assist in the garden (Fig. 5.23; see also Fig. 5.1).

During the initial planning stages, Steedman confessed ignorance about the fundamentals of gardening and also anticipated that the Casa grounds could be maintained by one man. Depending on one's perspective, he either was confronted with the reality of maintaining a property many times larger than he had in St. Louis, or he and his wife embraced the garden to a degree that they did not anticipate at first. Both positions are arguable. In 1930 Steedman developed the cutting garden specified in Stevens's original plan in meticulously detailed drawings indicating plant material (Figs. 5.24, 5.25). At the same time he laid out the semicircular "Rose and Dahlia" garden, a few steps below the east exedra (Fig. 5.26).[34] These drawings and surviving nursery invoices reveal the importance of flowers in the Casa garden. More than thirty varieties of roses were in evidence, fuschias were much in favor and hundreds of gladioli were planted annually, in addition to a wide assortment of other perennials and annuals. Steedman followed up in 1932 with a drawing for a so-called "western garden" below the garage court and indicated an assortment of herbs and other plants suited to a kitchen garden, though vegetables had been grown at the Casa since 1925 (Figs. 5.27, 5.28). The degree of Steedman's interest in these undertakings can be inferred from the labor he committed to them and from his surviving notes on plant propagation, soils, fertilizers, and pest control.

Joe Acquistapace (1902–1984) was head gardener at the Casa for forty-nine years. He took over from John Hartfeld, who was spirited away in 1930 by Dwight Murphy to serve as Park Superin-tendent for the City of Santa Barbara, and an interim replacement, David Greenwell. A member of a large Italian family, he started out as a gardener at Bernhard Hoffmann's house on Garden Street, moved on to the Milpas Nurseries in Santa Barbara and Santa Maria and also worked with Ralph Stevens and Peter Riedel. He began at the Casa in 1932 but there was an earlier family association: in the twenties laborers routinely cashed Casa paychecks at his cousin George Acquistapace's Eastern Market at 605 State Street. By 1934 Joe and his wife Amelia were living in the butler's cottage.[35]

Fifty years later, Joe recalled his experiences at the Casa in an oral history sponsored by the Santa Barbara Historical Museum. He supervised ten to twelve gardeners who worked six days a week and also oversaw constant redesigning of the garden:

> . . . Mrs. Steedman was quite a horticulturist, and I know when I went there in the thirties we tore that place all apart again. Not all of it, but different sections of it. Rebuilt the whole thing, and it's been that way ever since . . . the proper planting was done just perfect, and when it wasn't they came out and it was done over again—that's the way they were.

Acquistapace also mentioned participating in the many flower shows that were both Carrie Steedman's special interest and in which she frequently took honors, and a point of friendly local competition.

Fig. 5.24: Cutting garden with original brick paths bisecting the space.

Fig. 5.25: Cutting garden from south arbor.

Fig. 5.26: Rose and dahlia garden.

What I tried to do . . . See the McCormick estate had twenty or twenty-one gardeners, and they all thought that McCormick would come out first, which he always did. I'd go back and Mr. Steedman would want to know how I made out, and I'd go up and hand him all the ribbons and stuff, and he says, "You're going to get him!" And you know, I come pretty near to doing it, with just the few men I had. The difference is the knowledge, and knowing what to do and when to do it, that's the whole thing.[36]

A sort of brotherhood existed among the gardeners of the Montecito estates. They got together as a group from time to time and their activities were reported in *Modern Gardening*, published by the Santa Barbara County Horticultural Society. Joe's antics especially were deemed newsworthy. In 1938 the editor noted:

Joe Acquistapace was seen sailing through the air with the greatest of ease the other day. In guiding a tree to fall the rope took him right along, and boy you should have seen him. I believe he could do some stunts at our coming barbecue.

Figs. 5.27 and 5.28: Western garden.

*Fig. 5.29: Arthur Byne,
pepper tree fountain.*

*Fig. 5.30: Octagonal
pool and frog.*

FOLLOWING PAGES
Fig. 5.31: Peacock pool.

Fig. 5.32: Garden detail.

Fig. 5.33: Moorish watering trough.

FOLLOWING PAGES
Fig. 5.34: Cactus garden.

Two years later Joe was paraphrased as saying "if he had only known that the beautiful accordian [*sic*] player was going to talk with him he would have had all the answers ready, and might even have practiced up on 'Oh Johnny.' Joe says you know how it is when a good looking gal starts talking to you when you don't expect her to, it sort of leaves you speechless."[37]

In its heyday the garden exemplified the region's flourishing horticultural activity. A profusion of exotic plant material was available locally; to some extent the development of the great estates was responsible for a rise in the nursery business.[38] Several of the most prominent plantsmen supplied the Casa. Armstrong Nurseries in Ontario, one of the earliest and ultimately most important in Southern California, provided the initial plants.

E. O. Orpet was Superintendent of Parks in Santa Barbara between 1920 and 1930 and he also had experimental "trial grounds," six acres on Hollister Avenue. In 1924 he provided the Casa with a variety of flowers, yucca and banana plants and followed up in the thirties with specimen cacti and a wide variety of other succulents.[39] Theodore Payne, famous today for his California natives, similarly supplied the Casa.

Today the Casa garden is greatly simplified, particularly the cutting garden; much of the plant material used historically is no longer in evidence. Nonetheless, Ralph Stevens's basic design strategy and most of Steedman's changes and additions remain intact. The network of waterworks that originated with the fountain in the loggia parapet now begins with the star pool and continues underground a few feet when it resurfaces as a runnel feeding a small octagonal pool and then continues to a semicircular "peacock" pool, so named for its tile lining. The path continues underground to the

pepper tree fountain below (Figs. 5.29–5.31). Beyond and down several steps, a walled terrace with its padres' benches overlooks the cactus garden and Moorish watering trough below (Figs. 5.32–5.34).

Farther away from the house, the landscape has matured and in some areas become a forest Steedman could only have imagined. To the east, immense coast live oaks, conifers and the palm jungle display aged countenances of eight decades of growth (Fig. 5.35). The southern horizon is defined by orchards, eucalyptus trees, meandering paths, and arched openings, punctuated by an occasional red tile roof (Fig. 5.36).

Finally, there was another aspect of life in the Casa. The Steedmans were grandparents and the little ones descended from time to time and later, happily, recorded their impressions. First born was Margaret Hinckley (1929–), Katherine's daughter, who recalled visits between 1933 and 1941:

I assume my presence was welcomed by that august and orderly couple, although I'm sure they and I were happiest when I was "below stairs" rather than "above." I do not remember ever having been cuddled by either Granny or Grandfur or even hugged, but that did not seem strange, and it certainly did not detract from my viewing their habitation as being as close to heaven on earth as I was likely to get . . . .

When I was old enough to wander the grounds alone (although one was never really alone because there was almost always a gardener about . . .), I used to find a small flower or leaf and let it follow the tiny tiled channel that drained the star pool . . . .

If I continued on, I would walk very carefully through the cactus garden and on to the road that circled the orchards . . . . Then, if [brother] Steedman were with me, we might proceed on down into the wilds as far as the edifice of plaster and tile that served as "our" place and whatever we wanted it to be. Steedman and cousin George were allowed to spend the night there once or twice . . . .

At the height of the camellia season, Granny would have camellias all over the house; they were shown off best in the silver basins, low and tall, that Grandfur had made to display them . . . .

Sometimes I was allowed to accompany Granny when she cut the flowers each morning . . . . Then we would take the flowers into the shop, where she had her own corner filled with vases and scissors, and she would work miracles . . . . I really was more interested in what my grandfather's apprentice was doing. He usually did a lot of the design drawing for the wonderfully pictorial pieces of silver and pewter Grandfur turned out. Since we grandchildren occasionally featured in the scenes, I was often being drawn . . . .

There used to be an avocado grove that separated the front courtyard from the service courtyard and which provided a private forest in which

we could play. For hours on end Steedman and I would engage Harold and Lorraine Acquistapace (their father Joe was the head gardener and they lived in the house adjacent to the garages on the courtyard) in games that encompassed acres, it seemed, under the trees . . . .

The back courtyard of the house was the refuge of many a person laid low by the depression. Granny always had a supply of fruit there by the water basin for the ragged men to pick up, and sometimes cook would leave out some bread left over from the dining room table . . . .

The last discovery was the wine cellar, from the racks of bottles to the arcane accoutrements of wine making. I remember large carts of grapes being unloaded, and then processed by a means I either forgot or was not privileged to view, but I do remember the tables and the aroma . . . .

Grandfur was a man of many and diversified talents . . . and Granny was a more than adequate companion . . . while developing her own abilities. Casa del Herrero is a mirror of their devotion to excellence, balance and beauty . . . . [40]

Fig. 5.36: West opening from orchard to pepper tree fountain.

CHAPTER 6

A Good, Satisfying Home

I don't want anything showy, but I want it good.[1]

If there is one irrefutable fact about Casa del Herrero, it is that no detail escaped George Steedman's attention. And he was fearless in reworking both the house and the garden to carry out his ideas. The result is among the most thoughtful of houses and also one of the most personally expressive. Still, the catalyst for Steedman's determination remains elusive. He referred frequently to Spanish prototypes in his correspondence with George Washington Smith and others, though certainly he had Andalusian examples in mind and not Spanish architecture as a whole, which varies dramatically by region.[2] At the same time, his concept of Spanish taste is subject to interpretation: he seems to have been searching for the spirit rather than the letter, knowingly and willingly making concessions to time and place. What then, exactly, did he, Smith, Byne, and the others accomplish?

The short answer is a carefully calculated hybrid, beautiful in many aspects and far from unlovely overall, absent any negative connotations the term might suggest. Casa del Herrero might best be described as an admixture of farmhouse forms and palace opulence. Winsor Soule's book *Spanish Farmhouses and Minor Public Buildings*, published in 1924 and dismissed at the time by Steedman and Smith alike, in fact offers greater insight into the vernacular as expressed on the north elevation of the Casa than the better received *Provincial Houses in Spain* by Byne and Stapley, published in 1925. The south elevation is an early expression of Smith's interest in Italianate forms brought to conclusion in the grand Kirk Johnson house of 1928 on Sycamore Canyon Road.

Smith acknowledged to Byne in 1923 that in designing his Andalusian houses, he was "adapting the Spanish architecture to our American require-ments, and life in California." This synthetic quality was recognized early on by A. Lawrence Kocher, managing editor of *Architectural Record*, in a 1926 article on American country houses:

> . . . a few chosen styles dominate . . . . But these have been merged into designs that only faintly resemble the prototypes . . . .
>
> The Far West has played with the Spanish tradition for which in many ways it was well fitted by climatic conditions . . . . The architects . . . have gone far afield to combine with their native sources such borrowed elements as the Moorish, the Mexican, the Andalusian, and the South Italian . . . . The resulting style is their own, flexible because of the very variety of its elements . . . . They may speak Spanish, but it is with an accent all their own. Their country houses have the old world air, possibly, yet they are essentially a new creation . . . .
>
> The residence of Mr. George F. Steedman . . . is just such a composite house as I have indicated, Spanish only in essence. One would need to analyze it very minutely in order to determine its sources."[3]

Indeed, Casa del Herrero was assembled, so to speak, from many sources both primary and secondary. Smith like Steedman had firsthand exposure, having traveled through Spain in 1912 though there is scant record of his specific impressions. In addition the photographs he took in Spain in 1923, which he cited frequently as points of reference, Steedman made numerous sketches of details—not, significantly, larger architectonic aspects—that caught his eye and routinely suggested that Smith incorporate them into the Casa.[4] And the Bynes metaphorically and literally opened doors through which Steedman otherwise might not have passed.

The record also reveals frequent reference to published sources for design inspiration, both by Smith and Steedman. In July 1923, Smith wrote to Byne: "I think I have all your books and have found them a great help, especially your book on ceilings, which I have used quite a number of times." In June 1924 Steedman told Smith that he had "... spent the last three days analyzing Byne's [*sic*] book on decorated wooden ceilings, and am preparing some notes and designs . . . ." Smith followed up in a note to Byne of July 30, 1924: "I am very glad to hear that you are bringing out some more books. They are a great help."[5]

In addition to the Bynes' writings, Steedman and Smith turned to other publications for stylistic reference. Smith had in his office a copy of Austin Whittlesey's *The Minor Ecclesiastical Domestic and Garden Architecture of Southern Spain*, published in 1917, which was primarily a photographic resource. In 1924 Steedman called Smith's attention to a new book published by William Lawrence Bottomley, *Spanish Details*, which he described as "good on ceilings." For garden details Steedman relied on *Spanish & Portuguese Gardens* by Rose Standish Nichols,

published in 1924, and a series of articles collectively titled "Andalusian Gardens and Patios," by Byne and Stapley, that appeared in *Architectural Record* between December 1923 and September 1924.[6]

Ultimately Smith and Steedman trusted their own instincts. Their stylistic point of reference in designing the Casa seems to have been a combination of Spanish and Italian vernacular as revealed in the two main facades, north and south. The north front has the accidental composition of a Spanish farmhouse: simple geometric solids, planar white stucco surfaces, gabled tiled roofs and the ubiquitous lean-to. *Rejas* and the cast stone door surround provide typically chaste embellishment (Fig. 6.1). The south elevation is formal and basically symmetrical; a service wing is offset to the west. The dominant feature is a double arched loggia surmounted by an arcade. Another book in Smith's library, *Smaller Italian Villas* by Guy Lowell, published in 1916, included numerous variations on this type and may have provided the inspiration.[7]

If formal and stylistic analogy can be made— and direct antecedents traced—for the elevations

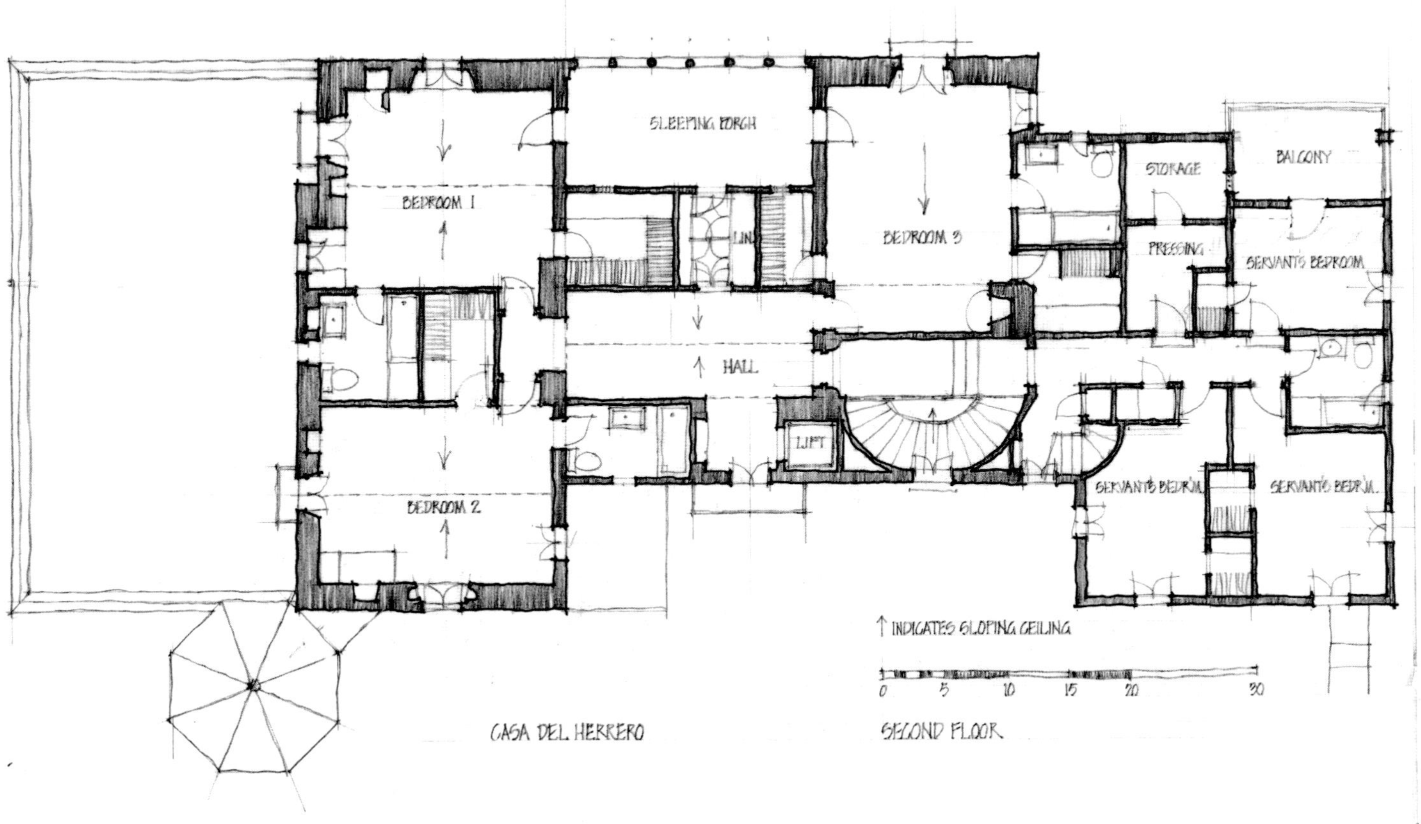

Fig. 6.2: Second floor plan.

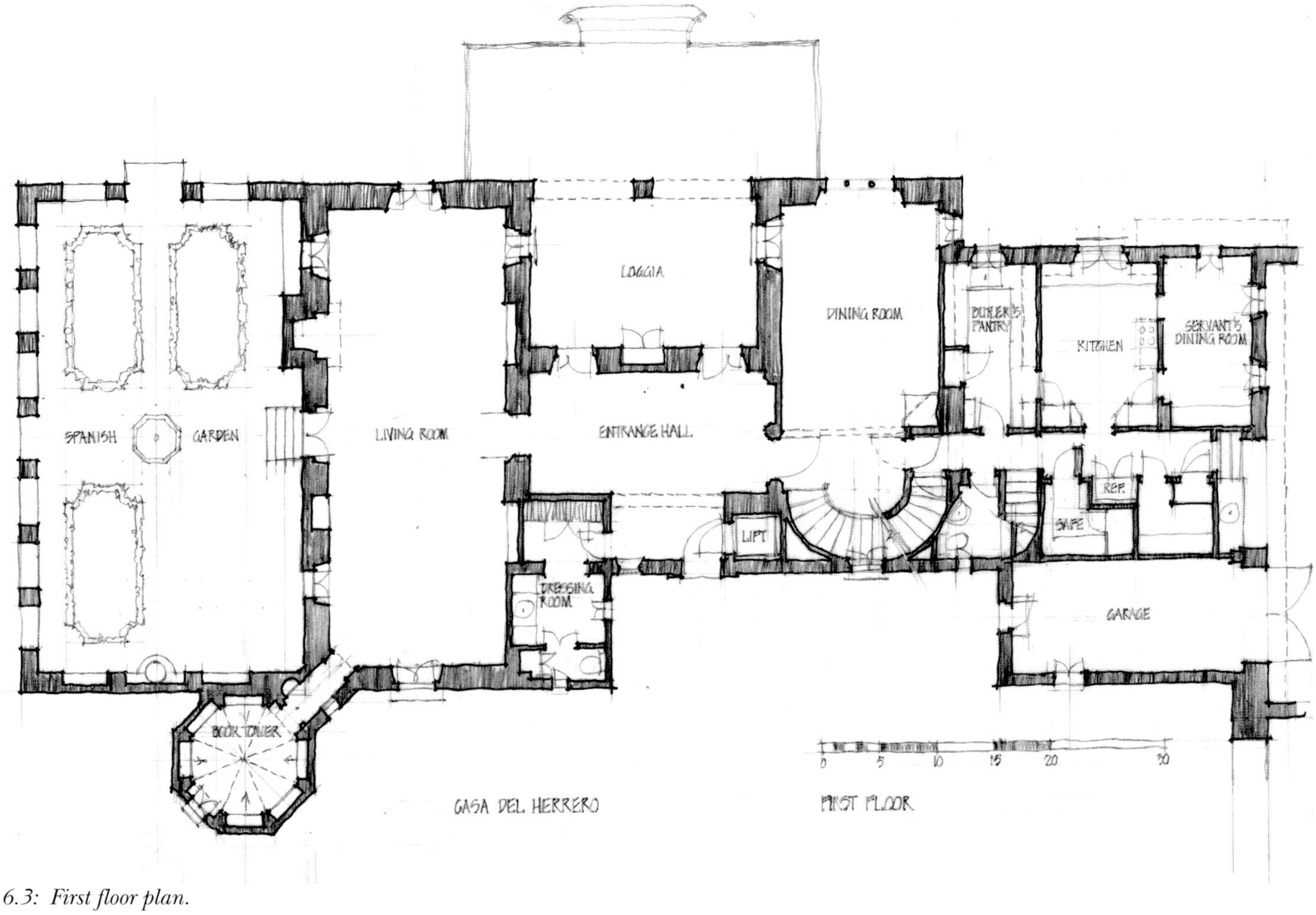

Fig. 6.3: First floor plan.

106

and details of the Casa, it is not possible to reconcile the floor plan with any historic prototype. The layout is unapologetically adapted to a twentieth-century lifestyle. Still there is undeniable formal and spatial resolution (Figs. 6.2, 6.3). In a nod to Spanish tradition and the local climate, living space continues outside in the loggia and Spanish garden (Figs. 6.6–6.8). Steedman later added the east exedra on an axis from the living room through the Spanish garden (Figs. 6.9, 6.10) and provided additional garden furniture (Figs. 6.11, 6.12).

Subtleties emerge on closer inspection. The house is dark, but the confines emphasize windows framing uplifting portraits of landscape and mountains in every direction. No visitor can leave without an indelible impression of the star pool with its gently rippling water and the vista beyond seen from the sleeping porch; this is the Casa's finest moment (Fig. 6.13). The paired doors split off center and opening from the entrance hall to the loggia are ingenious examples of woodworking with their inset shutters and endlessly fascinating array of hardware (Fig. 6.14). The pebble mosaic at the front entry which depicts the castle and lion of Ferdinand and Isabella and an eagle possibly symbolizing Habsburg rule in Spain reads most articulately when viewed from above. There are sly references to Steedman's name (STEED-man) and interest in metalworking, in the centaur relief over the main entry, in images painted by Channing Peake in the living room and on the dining room fireplace hood and in the cast reliefs on the pillars at the main entrance (Fig. 6.4). Further evidence of Steedman's playfulness appears in the oft-reworked living room fireplace: the women's heads supporting the hood were cast from a wooden original purchased in Paris in 1924 and now in his office. Menacing carved wood corbels lurk overhead to greet the unsuspecting as they ascend the main staircase (Fig. 6.5).

At the same time, it seems fair to acknowledge that Steedman's many changes over the years produced uneven aesthetic results. In general the work he undertook with professional advice is successful. Riggs's book tower is positioned skillfully as an adjunct to the mass of the house yet remains deferential in scale. The Italianate symmetry of the south elevation of the house was offset—made to seem more Spanish—with the addition of stone Catalan windows purchased in 1927 from Arthur Byne who advised: " . . . these two old windows would help to age Casa del Herrero immensely; furthermore they are dirt cheap . . . ."[8] The one below is a fine example of an *ajimez* or arched window with a column at the center; that above is Gothic.

Fig. 6.4: *Cast metal centaur, north entry gate.*

Fig. 6.5: *Carved wood corbel, second floor stair hall.*

Francis Underhill and Lockwood de Forest's garden structures establish points of reference and serve to frame spaces and views. They also add formality. De Forest's entrance court, especially, provides a stage for the house and enhances the ceremony of arrival.

Other of Steedman's changes, while seemingly opening and therefore simplifying spaces, did not have the intended effect. The parapet on the south side of the loggia provided an important point of termination, both spatially and formally. Its removal and replacement with open metal railings and axial semi-circular steps blurs the carefully calculated transition from indoor to outdoor space and visually weakens the south elevation as Smith envisioned it. Similarly, removing the steps at each end of the loggia destroyed clearly articulated paths of circulation to the herb garden on the west and the Spanish and cutting gardens to the east.

Also open to debate spatially and intellectually is the removal of the wall separating the dining room and stair hall. Albert Hinckley, Jr., recalls his grandmother justifying the decision because of an intolerable echo in the dining room. Mr. Hinckley also recounted a conversation with George Washington Smith's secretary who said that this change became a final wedge between Smith and Steedman.[9] The end result was an unorthodox combination of two ceremonial though functionally disparate spaces.

Fig. 6.8: George Steedman, 1937.

FACING PAGE
Figs. 6.9 and 6.10: Spanish garden.

FOLLOWING PAGES
Fig. 6.11: East exedra.

Less important though nonetheless intrusive are the various accretions to the butler's cottage. The new construction on the east and south facades obliterates the clarity of the original composition and reveals Steedman's willingness to compromise architectural integrity for pragmatic benefit.

If the design of the Casa itself can be attributed to many hands and sources, the interiors and furnishings reflect principally the seasoned taste of Arthur Byne and Mildred Stapley, as Steedman acknowledged:

> [We] were directed and guided by Mr. and Mrs. Arthur Byne of Madrid–All items . . . were purchased by the above parties . . . in nearly every case by unanimous approval of the four—and in no case was anything purchased without Mr. Bynes

[*sic*] advice and approval . . . . Mr. & Mrs. Byne . . . are the authors of the recognised [*sic*] books on Spanish art, architecture and furniture–and are the best known authorities on these subjects.[10]

Byne first discussed Spanish furniture in an article published in 1915. Speaking with surprising candor for such an advocate of Spanish culture, he disclaimed any true originality: " . . . a glance suffices to show that they adapted largely from other nations; but the point is that to every form they borrowed they imparted some characteristic touch that made the article forever after Spanish. This native touch expressed itself largely in the use of leather, in ornamental nail heads, and in iron bracing to the wooden framework of chairs and tables."[11]

In the text of the Bynes' three-volume *Spanish Interiors and Furniture*, published between 1922 and 1925, and in articles published in 1928, Stapley went on to describe the distinguishing peculiarities of Spanish furniture:

> The outstanding characteristic . . . is that it always remained masculine as opposed, for instance to French, which became feminine . . . . Furniture was designed chiefly for men—sturdy, serious fittings for monastery refectories, for council-rooms in castles and palaces, for studies, for banquet halls where, if women were admitted, it was not to sit on chairs at table with men but on cushions on the floor or in the deep window recesses where they were served apart . . . .
>
> Keeping this in mind we shall not expect to find light construction, woodwork hidden under gold and upholstered in pale evocative tones; nor concessions to femininity such as day-beds, commodes, specially designed dressing-tables . . . . In short, one would look in vain for a touch of *daintiness* in any genuine Spanish salon of the sixteenth or seventeenth century.

She also noted " . . . less nicety of craftsmanship" in comparison with the furniture of other countries and concluded, " . . . durability was esteemed paramount to finish . . . . "[12]

Continuing the pragmatic note, Stapley commented on the "thoroughly Spanish" attitude that " . . . ignored the exigencies of household service" and led to a " . . . failure to appreciate the superior practicability of bureaus, sideboards, dish-closets, escritoires, etc." She concluded:

> One may, then, in any brief review of Spanish furniture confine one's remarks to the following elementary objects: tables, chairs, benches, chests, vargueños (Spanish cabinet), beds. These, with the addition of picture and mirror frames, and of smaller objects like braziers, lanterns, candelabra, and a profusion of coffrets or table boxes, would make a representative list.[13]

Much of the Spanish furniture and art available to dealers and collectors in the early twentieth century was removed from monasteries and came on the market after the *Exclaustración*—Disestablishment Act—of 1835, which did away with religious orders and confiscated their property.[14] While the best pieces went into private collections much was lost because of ongoing political and economic reversal culminating with defeat in the Spanish-American war in 1898. After the war political and social strife increased and was further aggravated by World War I. The burgeoning interest in Spanish culture was aided—if not made possible by—this contemporary political climate.

By 1921 the Bynes were at the nucleus of the activity, as Stapley acknowledged to Julia Morgan:

> My husband went for a brief trip to N.Y. last January and made arrangements with several decorators there to send them complete Spanish interiors or separate pieces. We intended doing this only in a casual way, but the fact is we were almost overwhelmed with orders and have sent off a dozen large shipments since his return in March.

At about the same time the Bynes began acting as agents for William Randolph Hearst who was buying for his ". . . village on a mountain-top" at San Simeon; he ultimately became the largest purchaser of Spanish antiques though with time he became less interested in individual objects than " . . . bigger more architectural things."[15]

Soon enough Byne was reporting stiff competition. Writing shortly after Steedman had left Spain, he indicated that coveted pieces had been lost in Barcelona because of indecision but also that dealers had held things " . . . in the face of great temptation for . . . they were offered two and three times as much if they would resell." Back in Madrid he " . . . found great havoc had been wrought in the antique market. Addison Meizner [*sic*] the Palm Beach architect with several nouveau-riche clients had bought up over 200,000 pts [pesetas] worth of

115

stuff, most of it very poor, just stage setting. Still he cleaned the market and for your remaining things there is nothing to do but wait until the fall." Later Byne noted that John Wanamaker in Philadelphia also was buying heavily and recently had shipped 264 cases.[16]

Ultimately Steedman's own purchases filled more than 160 containers that were shipped from Spain between 1923 and 1928.[17] It probably is not possible to fully sort out the various items, from whom he acquired them or the costs. He prepared several handwritten inventories that are contradictory and the simplified "consular invoices" prepared for shipping the goods from Spain further cloud the issue. Also, given measurements that might lead to identification of similar items are imprecise; some items listed on the inventories seem not to be in the Casa today; conversely, other items are present which cannot be reconciled with the documentation.

To keep track of purchases made in 1923–24 Steedman organized the furniture and other objects by category—tables, chairs, benches and stools, chests, etc., a format Stapley adopted in her writings—and assigned a code to each piece indicating point of origin. The pieces for which dates are indicated are generally from the fifteenth to the eighteenth centuries though the bulk is from the 1600s and a few are nineteenth century. There also are modern reproductions.

Steedman's most important acquisition was the requisite decorated ceiling, or *artesonado*, that he bought for the Casa entrance hall from Byne in 1923 (Figs. 6.14, 6.15). Byne explained its provenance:

> The monastic house from which your XV-century ceiling came is, or rather was, el Convento de San Francisco, near the town of Darroca [*sic*: Daroca], in the Province of Teruel, once part of the old Kingdom of Aragón. Like many other monasteries it was fired by the Liberal mobs in the anti-monastic uprisings of 1835. Your ceiling is all that remains of the covering to the old claustral walk. Not until you see the ceiling will you appreciate the time I have had with it. If I had sent it over "as was" it would have been a Chinese puzzle and a costly one to solve. As arranged now you will have nothing to do but slip the panels in place.[18]

The ceiling consists of forty-eight painted wood panels—small pictures—recessed in frames supported on open beams fourteen inches on center (Fig. 6.16). Transverse decorated strips between the beams separate the panels. In addition there are thirty-two panels carved with Mudejar stars used as borders. Most of the depictions are figural though there are a few panels of pure decoration.

The painted panels are bordered by white or red dots on black; these in turn are usually surrounded by a red or ochre foliate motif on a black ground. The scored beams are near copies of the originals, most of which were in poor condition and could not be reused (Fig. 6.16). Those few that were salvageable were placed in the beauty parlor with plain panels between.[19]

Stapley elaborated on the symbolic and artistic significance of this ceiling in an article published in 1927. She described a combination of ". . . floral and geometric *motifs* so characteristic of the art of Islam but also with Christian compositions of figures and animals, such as Gothic Europe was then demanding in its tapestries, sculptures, and paintings." Stylistically the paintings derive from the ceiling of Teruel Cathedral—the finest remaining example in situ—and are primarily religious in theme though there also are scenes from daily life and occasional grotesques. All in all they present a fascinating record of the people, costumes and mythology of the time.[20]

Steedman's ceiling is related to two others of similar provenance, though the structural framing

is not the same. One was purchased from Byne by William Randolph Hearst in 1925 and installed in his bedroom at San Simeon. It is hipped with the painted panels installed on the sloping sides, unlike Steedman's which is framed with open horizontal beams. The other was purchased by Myron C. Taylor, at the time a director and member of the finance committee of United States Steel, from the collection of the Duke of Almenas at auction in 1927 and installed in Villa Schifanoia, located north of Perugia in Umbria. It is similarly hipped but with sixty-four (originally seventy-eight) panels, making it the largest of the three.[21]

Many of the shutters Steedman purchased were intended originally for unglazed openings and incorporate a separate hinged panel to mitigate the intense light, heat and cold in Spain. The old Spanish doors acquired for the house are the typical lightweight but "structurally complicated" assemblages of "an infinite number of geometric panels mortised and tenoned together," Stapley described. Most notable is a seventeenth-century Mudejar door and frame from Ecija, a type suggested by Smith and installed in the second floor hall (Fig. 6.17). Another important door was the one removed from the sacristy of a church in Étretat and now in the book tower. Its immediate provenance notwithstanding, the nature of the carving has led several observers to speculate on possible Mexican origin, but Steedman described it as "Breton . . . in the antique style—gothic or even romanesque [*sic*]—and while not Spanish, will harmonize with Spanish–" (see Fig. 4.23). He initially suggested using it in the beauty parlor but it was first hung over a niche in the living room.[22]

Tables (*mesas*) and chairs are the most numerous items on Steedman's inventories. Most of the tables available for sale came from monasteries and were of two general types: those with turned legs set vertically and, more commonly, with splayed legs of waved or lyre form. Wooden stretchers stiffened the turned legs; ornamental iron braces were used with splayed legs. Both types had thick walnut slab tops and were made with and without drawers. They often were ingeniously designed to be demountable; the center table in the south end of the living room is an example.

Silla is the collective word for chair in Spanish; the so-called *frailero* or monk's chair was the predominating type. It had a simple open wooden frame with a leather seat and back attached with hand-finished iron or brass nails. Steedman purchased fourteen of these from a convent in Palma, of which seven are now in the second-floor hall of the Casa (Fig. 6.32; see also 6.17). The addition of luxurious fabrics and metal mountings elevated

these originally straightforward objects to another level; several examples are in the entry hall and living room.[23] Steedman also purchased several wood frame chairs with upholstered seats and high backs that are a derivation of a type common in central Europe.

The red and green painted chairs in the dining room represent another type that was used with variations in many parts of Spain. These, from Catalonia, have the rush seats preferred in the region (Figs. 6.25, 6.27). Stapley referred to them as " . . . cottage types show[ing] considerable skill in their simple surface adornment . . . . The provinces are ransacked for them and side by side with their modern facsimiles they are placed in the same salon with rich damask hangings, velvet-covered furniture, and precious works of art of all kinds; the distinction they would have in a simple interior is thus lost."[24]

Benches (*bancos*) were ubiquitous in Spain. Steedman bought several which can be seen in the beauty parlor, sleeping porch, and shop. Low stools (*banquetes*) similarly were widely used. They typically had turned legs and are most interesting for the S-shaped saw-cuts in the seats that facilitate picking them up. Most of Steedman's stools are reproductions built by Arthur Byne.

Chests were the principal storage units in Spain but they also served as tables and, with the addition of cushions, as seating. They were often covered in leather attached with ornamental nails. Stapley observed in 1922, "In unpretentious rural houses it is not unusual to encounter even today as many as thirty old chests and not a single bureau," though in the Casa their role and number are limited.[25]

Again in 1922 Mildred Stapley identified the *vargueño* as ". . . the preeminently Castilian piece of furniture." She continued, ". . . in spite of the great number that have been sold they are still seen everywhere." A *vargueño* is essentially a wooden box with numerous small drawers and compartments resting on a separate base. It has a hinged front that opens to provide a writing surface and typically is decorated with ornamental pierced iron in great variety and degree of richness; the pieces tend to be as decorative as they are utilitarian. A variation without the hinged front is called a *papelera*. Steedman purchased both types; a *vargueño* is in the living room, a pair of *papeleras* in the entrance hall (Fig. 6.20). Bases could be tables or cabinets; a *vargueño* with a cabinet is analogous to an English or American fall-front secretary. Most common was a trestle stand with built-in sliding supports for the hinged front as seen at the Casa.[26]

124

Fig. 6.17: Ecija door, second-floor hall.

In addition to the stools acquired from Byne, modern pieces include three sets of painted furniture—red, yellow, and black—purchased in Seville for the servants' rooms. Marshall Laird in Los Angeles built the living room sofa and beds for Carrie Steedman's and the guest bedrooms. Laird also fabricated several doors for the Casa including the one for the main entry, and he corrected the dimensions of the antique doors and shutters.[27]

George Steedman and Louis La Beaume capped off their shopping and sightseeing odyssey in Spain with three small exhibitions at the City Art Museum of St. Louis, as it was then called. Steedman loaned the tapestries purchased in Paris to the museum in December 1923. One, the Flemish religious scene, was displayed the following year alongside another Flemish tapestry depicting a late gothic allegorical romance. Both were described in the museum *Bulletin* as studio designs; i.e., products of a highly organized industry that had developed in Flanders by the end of the fifteenth century, in which the tapestries were worked on by a number of specialized assistants under the direction and from the sketches of one head master (see Fig. 6.14).

A Selection of Spanish Decorative Arts from the Collection of Louis La Beaume followed in November 1925. Museum records from this period are incomplete and no exhibition checklists have been located; however, a letter from La Beaume to Steedman of November 30, 1925, offers some clarification. La Beaume refers to "Our Spanish show," indicating Steedman's participation, and told Steedman he would "hold your items . . . for packing . . . . " A parallel exhibition, Water Colors by Arthur Byne, was shown November 17–30.[29] This was a group of twenty-seven views of Spain and Majorca, some of which presumably would have been familiar to readers of *Architectural Record*.

Steedman continued buying furniture and other objects from Arthur Byne for several more years, seemingly against considerable odds. On August 15, 1926, the Spanish government enacted a law restricting exportation of cultural artifacts.[30] But even before official intervention Byne encountered opposition and established a pattern of shadowy maneuvering out of character with the image he generally presented. In early 1926, after several articles appeared in the Spanish press condemning William Randolph Hearst's purchase of a

monastery, Byne gave a chilling account of the circumstances:

> Fortunately the owner of the Monastery is one of the foremost figures in the present Military Dictatorship. It is part of the agreement that he crush all such criticism from the press (and as there is still a final payment of $10,000 coming to him when the whole operation is over, you may be assured that he does it). But it's no easy job. Everyone along the line, from the simplest country official in the vicinity of the site, to the station masters, the highway police, the freight people, the harbor inspectors, and the steamship officials, all must be hushed with money. This money coming from me but distributed by men in my employ. It is not a pleasant thing to relate but it is the only way an undertaking of this magnitude can be managed.[31]

In fact, the stripping of Spain's cultural artifacts had been discussed much earlier, frequently by the Bynes themselves. Mildred Stapley raised the topic in 1914 in a discussion of Talavera pottery:

> Being determined to possess a few specimens of this famous pottery I asked for it in every antique dealer's we saw in Spain. The answer was always the same: "Ah, señora, you stand more chance of picking up a piece in Paris or London than in Spain. After the Napoleonic war had opened up the peninsula to foreigners, French and English dealers came down and carried off everything.[32]

Byne revisited the theme the next year:

> Spanish craftsmen made some very beautiful furniture during the Middle Ages and the Renaissance, though not much remains in Spain today to prove the fact. A long list of Spanish political disturbances caused the looting and destroying of many a fine mansion; French and English antique dealers invaded the land and took innumerable works of art back to Paris and London with them; then Spanish antique dealers, called into being by the former, scoured the country and were still able to collect enough portable objects to stock their shops in such tourist centers as Madrid, Granada and Sevilla.[33]

Stapley took yet another shot in her 1926 book *Forgotten Shrines of Spain*:

> No praise would be too extravagant for the Covarrubias triptych, nor for the exquisite little painting of the Madonna that hangs in the sacristy. Of this we took a photograph, the first and only one ever made of it . . . . Both these treasures, the triptych and the painting, being now published and thereby saved from the antiquaries, it must cause them to gnash their teeth in rage when they pass through the place.[34]

Clearly the Bynes wished to distance themselves from the frenzy and avariciousness. In a 1921 letter to Julia Morgan, Stapley commented, "Many things are brought to our attention to be quietly sold that would never reach the ordinary dealer, and our

good judgment and fair dealing stand high both with the seller and the purchaser." Byne followed up defensively two months later, " . . . no one in all Spain is in touch with salable treasures to the extent that we are, and we ask less profit on any transaction than the rapacious professional antiquarians."[35] These statements aside, the inescapable reality is that the Bynes—and to some extent their

Figs. 6.18 and 6.19: Living room/Arab doors.

receptive clients—were actively engaged in the pillaging.

Purchases of Spanish antiquities for the Casa continued until 1930. The choir stalls in the entry were added in 1926; Byne described them as " . . . the best of Spanish XV century Gothic" (see Fig. 6.14). In January 1927 Steedman bought several pieces from

Fig. 6.20: Living room/vargueño.

take advantage of this opportunity. Byne was not tentative in describing the collection, noting:

> Nothing so important in medieval and early Renaissance art will ever again come out of Spain, not only because an equal number of genuine objects of the same range and high quality could never again be assembled, but because of the recent law of August fifteenth, 1926, against their exportation is now rigorously enforced and would prevent their being offered *en bloc* to connoisseurs.[36]

Steedman purchased five lots from the Almenas sale, most notably a sixteenth-century polychromed wood statue by Alonso Berruguete, the greatest sculptor of the Spanish Renaissance who possibly studied under Michelangelo or at least was influenced by him. The statue, identified as Padre Eterno, stands sentry today in the Casa entrance hall (Fig. 6.15). Byne described the piece:

> The *Padre Eterno* is a standing figure three-quarters life size, of great dignity, recalling the impressiveness of Michael Angelo's statues. The weight, resting on the right hip, gives a pleasing curve to the body. The right hand is raised in benediction and the left holds the globe of the antique world, meaning the globe of the pre-discovery epoch when Christianity spread of Asia, Africa and Europe only. On the head is an elaborate crown with jeweled band and surmounted by a gold ball. The face, while of the general patriarchal type, shows close study from a very interesting living model. The long dark tunic is caught in at the waist by a knotted girdle, and the mantle, which retains much of its gold, is pushed well to the back. The polychromy in general is in excellent condition.[37]

The sixteenth-century alabaster statue of St. George, also in the entry, came from the Almenas sale as well.

Later in 1927 Steedman bought an extension table for the dining room from Arthur Byne, who explained its significance:

> These tables come from the Alta Aragon, in the ridges and valleys of the Pyrenees. In no other part of Spain were they ever made. French and Italian influence in the design is manifest. I organized an expedition that went through this primitive region and we succeeded in bagging eight examples. In two instances, because the mountain passes were so narrow, the tables had to be completely taken [a]part to get them out of the village. In another instance, tho the village is Spanish, the table was carted out on the French side their [*sic*] being absolutely no means of getting in nor out of the hamlet on the Spanish side!

the collection of José María de Palacio y Abárzuza, Conde de las Almenas, Madrid, at a forced sale in New York. Byne seems to have been acting as agent to sell the collection as early as 1925; Julia Morgan expressed interest in buying items individually on Hearst's behalf. Steedman had seen the collection in 1923 and Byne, who with his wife, wrote the descriptions for the sale catalogue, urged him to

He concluded that Steedman's table was "in a class with the several exhibited in the Museum des Arts

Décoratifs, in Paris. It is in beautiful condition and not expensive" (see Fig. 6.27).

The Arab doors in the living room at the passage from the entry hall were acquired in 1928. Steedman bought them with " . . . qualms of conscience . . . " because of the cost; Byne responded, "When you see the doors you will agree with me that you don't possess anything finer . . . . " In fact, like so much of the Casa furniture, they were heavily restored (Figs. 6.18, 6.19). Byne explained:

> For years they were in the collection of that old Belgium in Granada, who has so many fine things. I bought them at a stiff price and once in Madrid set about cleaning them. You may think you did some cleaning but it was not a patch on what we took off–the whitewash of ages. As so often happens in cases of that sort once one removes indefinite coats of wash or paint some surprises are revealed underneath. I had to restore completely some of the <u>lacería</u> [diagonal interlacing] and take most of it off and put it on again. But what disturbed most was that the original metal bands around the pivots at the top and bottom had disappeared (stolen by gypsies I suppose) and tin ones replaced at a later date. It broke my heart to send the doors off with those miserable bands but as I had no time to make bronze ones I had to let it go.[39]

Steedman spent seven years furnishing the Casa; he considered it complete in 1930. Thanking Steedman for a payment on April 20, Byne continued:

> The seven years that are [*sic*] account has been running have been interesting to me. And I hope that our correspondence will continue just the same even though the orders are all filled!

The next year Steedman commissioned Fred Dapprich, a Los Angeles photographer, to make a photographic record. Dapprich's images reflect overall sumptuousness but stiff arrangements of furniture—in Spanish tradition—along the walls, particularly in the living room. Also in Spanish tradition there seems to have been, in Stapley's words, " . . . no instance of concession to creature comfort."[40]

Stapley described the characteristics of a traditional Spanish house at length in her essay for *Spanish Interiors and Furniture*, identifying "lordly XVI-century palace interiors" and "modest rural seats of old well-to-do families" as the "most truly national because their dominating note is . . . the *Mudéjar* or combined Moorish and Christian." The distinguishing features, which she termed "built-in decoration," were " . . . a free use of glazed ceramic in the form of polychrome tiles [and] a carved and painted wooden ceiling with doors and inside shutters of similar carpentry . . . . " Finally, she identified characteristic "great spaces of white wall [that] were appreciated for their decorative contrast to the occasional hangings . . . of great variety" and commented, "It is surprising how an apartment of such unmitigated . . . simplicity can be transformed into something very sumptuous by a few dignified pieces of furniture, a few metal lamps suspended

on long chains, and a few silk or tapestry hangings" (Fig. 6.21). She also issued a note of caution:

> Collectors in Spain, like those the world over, have found the temptation to crowd the house irresistible . . . . To do this . . . does not result in that tranquil, spacious interior, which is the tradition of Spain.[41]

If George Steedman did indeed succumb to temptation, the effect at the Casa may have more to do with scale and proportion than profusion of objects. Much of the Spanish furniture he purchased was designed for loftier spaces; the living room ceiling, especially, seems low (Fig. 6.24).

Fig. 6.21: Stair hall/brass hanging church lamp.

129

Steedman acknowledged this after Byne offered him a fourteenth-century frieze, telling Smith, "It looks most attractive but after studying the possibilities I had to conclude we could not use it as our ceilings are too low . . . . " He lamented, "I do wish our ceilings were high enough . . . to take it–and it would have been so simple if I had been willing to have the big simple room at first–."[42]

The dining room with its Aubusson tapestry more nearly approaches the tranquility Stapley described. It was changed dramatically when the wall separating the stair hall was removed. Space expanded horizontally and vertically and new points of reference were established (Figs. 6.26, 6.28, 6.29; see also Fig. 6.27). In the same vein, the three bedrooms and sleeping porch upstairs have pitched ceilings and are arguably more spatially uplifting than the public rooms on the first floor, though architects may note that the slope of the ceilings does not consistently follow the roofline above.

131

Figs. 6.25–6.27
(following pages):
Dining room.

*Fig. 6.28: Staircase
with Chemla tile risers.*

Fig. 6.29: Staircase.

As in many great houses, the service areas are of no small interest. The butler's pantry, kitchen, servants' dining room and back stair all received their share of tile embellishment and hanging lamps (Figs. 6.30, 6.31).

Arthur Byne and Mildred Stapley stopped at the Casa in 1930 en route to the east coast after a visit to Hearst's San Simeon. One wishes in vain that Stapley had recorded her impressions of the interiors though undoubtedly she never would. Byne was more forthcoming. Back in Madrid, he wrote to Steedman about the Casa garden, which he concluded was "the one weak spot in the whole enterprise." In his opinion it was " . . . very messy, there is no scheme, and no amount of little tinkering will ever help it." He sent three sketches, suggesting simplification and stating:

> The scheme in its ensemble must be that of a cruciform. Your long vista presents a great opportunity and must be developed to its limit. It is equally important though that the cross arm be accentuated, distinctly, but at the same time giving way to the long arm in importance.

Fig. 6.30: Back stair.

*Fig. 6.31: Servants'
dining room.*

Byne indicated that his schemes were not perfect but had the " . . . merit of being direct and simple." He invited Steedman to add " . . . all the detail you wish in the way of planting, but don't lose track of the general idea. I know this will be hard for you to resist once you get busy with your pencil and rubber. You remind me exactly of my father; he appreciates the simplified thing when it is shown to him but by the time he has 'perfected' it little remains of the simplicity."[43]

PREVIOUS PAGES
Fig. 6.32: Second-floor hall.

Fig. 6.33: Carrie Steedman bedroom.

Fig. 6.34: Wall safe with old painted doors and modern surround decorated by Channing Peake, ca. 1933–34.

FOLLOWING PAGES
Fig. 6.35: George Steedman bedroom.

Five years later Arthur Byne was killed at age 50 in a motor accident near Santa Cruz de Mudela, Spain. Writing to Mildred Stapley a short time afterward, George Steedman displayed a heartfelt generosity of spirit:

> I spend my daily life with the things that you and he helped me to purchase over ten years ago and remember so often the very happy few weeks I spent with you and your husband in Spain . . . .
>
> It really is a very intimate association to have all of your most prized possessions . . . remind you of the good taste and high ideals of life which you and Mr. Byne possessed. You helped me to make a very happy home here in California. It is not a museum—it is just a good, satisfying home. I can say without any exaggeration that I shall always remember Arthur Byne in connection with it.[44]

Fig. 6.36: Girls' bedroom.

Fig. 6.37: Girls' bedroom window detail.

FACING PAGE
Fig. 6.38 Carrie Steedman bathroom.

Fig. 6.39: George Steedman bedroom.

CHAPTER 7

Change

On March first, 1940, Gordon Grant suffered a gruesome injury in the Casa shop. According to newspaper reports, he was looking down the muzzle of a functioning and loaded miniature canon, when his cigarette ignited the powder train. The "'canon ball,' a quarter-inch ball bearing, entered Grant's right eye and went deep into his brain." He died three hours later at Cottage Hospital.[2]

Eight weeks later, on April 28, George Fox Steedman died at the Casa. His funeral was in St. Louis; his ashes were deposited at Bellefontaine Cemetery.[3] Carrie Steedman lived on at the Casa until her death there twenty-two years later, in 1962. She left it as it was with one exception. In 1957 she replaced the solid wooden shutters over the arcaded openings in the sleeping porch with glazed casement windows that remain in place today.[4]

Carrie Steedman also retained a loyal—if greatly reduced—staff, some of whom bridged the transition of ownership to the Steedmans' daughter Medora Bass. Clarence Baker, who was hired as chauffeur in 1932 and witnessed Gordon Grant's accident in the shop, remained until 1946. Joe Acquistapace continued on until 1981, assuming temporary responsibilities as Casa chicken farmer during World War II. George Bass, the Steedmans' grandson, recalled in 2003:

> . . . my grandmother had chickens here. They were in the small front house where they start plants for the garden, but in order to maintain help here during the war time they had to prove there was something agricultural going on. So she got some chickens . . . .[5]

Ildo C. Marra (1922–1996) summarily replaced Baker in 1948 though by then the job descriptions were becoming blurred; he took over as chief factotum on Joe's retirement. Baker, Acquistapace, and Marra all raised families at the Casa, as John Hartfeld and William Hart had earlier; in every case their children have returned with recollections.

Provision was made in 1936 for the Casa to go to Medora Steedman Bass; title passed to her on Carrie Steedman's death.[6] Medora and her husband George used it part time until they moved there permanently in 1977; he died at the Casa in 1985.[7] Early the next year Mrs. Bass attended a meeting of the Montecito History Committee to discuss the future of the Casa. She expressed the desire to keep her family's property "as it is" and made an extraordinary offer: she would be willing to give the property to an organization that was able to keep it up.[8] She followed up in much the same vein in a circular letter written a few months later:

> For the past year, I have been receiving input on how best to leave my property to our community. The comments have been very helpful in focusing my thoughts and enabling me to come to some conclusions . . . .
>
> I wish to donate my property to a non-profit foundation or institution as soon as possible . . . .
>
> I wish to be involved in shaping the indoor and outdoor programs that will ultimately take place at the property, subject to the limitations desired by the neighbors and Montecito.
>
> I wish the property to remain intact as a community asset . . . .
>
> I am not interested in prejudging the programming as long as it is educational and/or inspirational . . . .

Lotusland, The Santa Barbara Historical Society, City College, and the Montecito Foundation have all expressed some interest.[9]

In an ideal situation, Mrs. Bass probably would have given the Casa to Planned Parenthood, an organization on whose board she served in Philadelphia and whose mission she trumpeted with extraordinary outspokenness in contrast to the well-bred demeanor she projected in other circumstances. But Planned Parenthood had neither real use for the property nor ability to support it financially.[10]

Negotiations with Santa Barbara City College proceeded in detail but without resolution during Mrs. Bass's lifetime. She died on December 5, 1987, leaving a living trust with her children George (1931–) and Medora (1941–) as trustees.[11] Although an agreement to transfer the property from the trust to the Foundation for Santa Barbara City College was drafted in April 1988, and the gift was announced in the press, discussion ended two years later, in April 1990.[12]

Several months earlier the trust had entered into negotiations with the Santa Barbara Historic Society. Mrs. Bass had made an overture to the society in 1987, before discussions with the college began, expressing an interest in having the Casa become a museum. Although the dialogue with the Historic Society continued optimistically for three years, and several drafts of a transfer agreement were prepared, the gift finally was declined for financial reasons.

A self-described entrepreneur, George Bass decided to abandon the idea of institutional affiliation and instead to establish a private foundation for the Casa. In 1993 he engaged Laura Bridley as a planning consultant to assist in obtaining the essential conditional use permit. Laura worked between January and August with the Montecito Association Land Use Committee, on which she and Dan Eidelson served; she also met with neighbors to get their support. The CUP was issued by the Planning Commission in November, on the recommendation of the Montecito Association.

All the while, George Bass was seeking funding; it was not initially his intention to invest his own money in the project. When he realized that financial support was not forthcoming, he reconsidered:

> So finally I looked at what I had – Grandpa gave me this money; I'd better give it back to him . . . . So there was some money from Mother and some money from me . . . . [13]

Medora Bass, George's sister, made a handsome gift of money as well.

Casa del Herrero opened to the public in June 1995, eight years after the death of Medora Bass. In the interim the house sat furnished but unoccupied. Much of the original furniture and decorative art had been extensively rearranged and in some cases placed in closets and in the basement; also, items had been added that were inconsistent with the original intentions. Mrs. Bass had used the sleeping porch an office; it was filled with her papers. Using the 1931 Dapprich photographs as a guide, most of the objects in the house were restored to their original positions and nonconforming accretions were removed.[14]

The garden was completely overgrown. A committee including Edward Hartfeld, son of the first gardener, and who was born in the gardener's cottage in 1923, was formed to cut back the overgrowth and to return the garden as closely as possible to its appearance at the time of Carrie Steedman's death.[15]

Since 1994 various restoration projects have been completed on the Casa, the gardener's and butler's cottages, the shop, the eastern exedra and the glass and lath houses near the western property line. While much remains to be accomplished, and all work is dependent on securing funding, there is reason for optimism.

On February 16, 2009, Secretary of the Interior Dirk Kempthorne announced the designation of Casa del Herrero as a National Historic Landmark. One of only four sites in Santa Barbara to be so acknowledged—the Mission, the Santa Barbara County Courthouse, and the Rafael Gonzalez house are the others—the designation ". . . is the highest such recognition accorded by the nation to historic properties determined to be of exceptional value in representing or illustrating an important theme, event, or person in the history of the nation."[16]

George Fox Steedman must be proud.

FOLLOWING PAGES
Fig. 7.1: Eastern garden.

NOTES

Unless noted, all correspondence cited is in the George Washington Smith Papers, Architecture and Design Collection, University Art Museum, University of California, Santa Barbara. Other correspondence comes from the archives of Casa del Herrero, identified as Casa, and from the Julia Morgan Papers, Special Collections, University Archives, California Polytechnic State University, San Luis Obispo, identified as Morgan Papers.

CHAPTER ONE
A Taste for Things Spanish

1. Louis La Beaume, "A Little Tour in Spain," *Journal of the American Institute of Architects* 12, no. 2 (February 1924): 47. Other articles in the series appeared in April, September, and November 1924 and March and October 1925.

2. *A History of the Hispanic Society of America Museum and Library 1904–1954. With a Survey of the Collections* (New York: Hispanic Society of America, 1954), ix. Susan Rosenstein, The Hispanic Society of America, to author, June 6, 2007. "Chas. P. Huntington Dies," *New York Times*, October 16, 1919. "Huntington, Charles Pratt," *American Art Annual* 16 (1919): 221. "Obituary [Charles Pratt Huntington]," *American Architect* 116, no. 2292 (November 26, 1919): 666. "A. M. Huntington, a Philanthropist," *New York Times*, December 12, 1955. "Art Patron Memorialized," *New York Times*, December 20, 1955.

3. Nancy R. Miller, Archivist, University of Pennsylvania, to author, February 6, 2007.

4. "Mrs. Arthur Byne, Authority on Art," *New York Times*, December 25, 1941. Mildred Stapley, "Is Paris Wise for the Average American Girl?" *Ladies' Home Journal* 23, no. 5 (April 1906): 16, 54. Mildred Stapley, "The K. and A. Company," *St. Nicholas* 34, no. 7 (May 1907): 612–16. Mildred Stapley, "Elsie's Lesson," *St. Nicholas* 35, no. 6 (April 1908): 507–11. Arthur G. Bein, "A Day in Williamsburg," *American Architect* 95, no. 1749 (June 30, 1909): 209–14.

5. Mildred Stapley, "Arthur Byne's Renderings and Water-colors," *Architectural Record* 47, no. 5 (May 1920): 425. George Edmund Street, *Some Account of Gothic Architecture in Spain* (London: John Murray, 1865).

6. M. Stapley, "Spanish Grilles," *American Architect* 99, no. 1838 (March 15, 1911): 97–100, 102–03.

7. Arthur G. Byne, "Where a Spanish Artist Lived: House of El Greco," *American Architect* 99, no. 1841 (April 5, 1911): 125–28. G. W. Smith and his client, Mrs. Bryce, were likewise enthusiastic about the house.

8. Victoria Rodríguez Thiessen, "Byne and Stapley: Scholars, Dealers, and Collectors of Spanish Decorative Arts" (master's thesis, Cooper-Hewitt, National Design Museum and Parsons School of Design, 1998), 5.

9. Stapley, "Arthur Byne's Renderings and Water-Colors" 425.

10. Bertram G. Goodhue, "Of Spanish and Mexican Themes," *Architectural Record* 38, no. 1 (July 1915): 187–89. Marrion Wilcox, "The Famous Ironwork of Spain," *Architectural Record* 39, no. 5 (May 1916): 491–93.

11. Marrion Wilcox, "Hispanic Society Publications," *Architectural Record* 43, no. 5 (May 1918): 481–84. William Lawrence Bottomley, "Review of 'Decorated Wooden Ceilings in Spain,'" *Architectural Record* 51, no. 6 (June 1922): 542–43. The book was published by G. P. Putnam's Sons, New York and London, as part of the Hispanic Society's Hispanic Notes and Monographs series. Information on Bottomley's friendship with Byne is in Byne to Steedman, September 12, 1923, Casa.

12. President, Hispanic Society of America, to Byne, December 30, 1918. Cited in Thiessen, "Byne and Stapely."

13. Huntington, January 4, 1919. Cited in Thiessen, "Byne and Stapely." While much research on the Bynes remains to be done, it may be useful to respond briefly to Huntington's assessment. The Bynes did seem intent on buffing their image. He was born Arthur Bein; he changed his name to Byne in 1910. Also, Stapley was his senior by nine years. Perhaps because of this, they routinely adjusted their ages on travel documents. In the most extreme instance, in 1913, he added eleven years while she deducted six. List of United States Citizens (for the Immigration Authorities).

14. Stapley to Huntington, August 18, 1919. Cited in Thiessen, "Byne and Stapely."

15. Thiessen, "Byne and Stapely," 8.

16. Bertram Grosvenor Goodhue, "The Architecture and the Gardens.," in Carleton Monroe Winslow, et al., *The Architecture and the Gardens of the San Diego Exposition* (San Francisco: Paul Elder and Company, 1916), 4. Richard Oliver, *Bertram Grosvenor Goodhue* (New York: The Architectural History Foundation, and Cambridge, Massachusetts, and London, England: The MIT Press, 1983), 118.

17. Bertram G. Goodhue, *Mexican Memories: The Record of a Slight Sojourn below the Yellow Rio Grande* (New York: G. M. Allen Company, 1892). Sylvester Baxter, *Spanish-colonial Architecture in Mexico* (Boston: J. B. Millet, 1901).

18. Oliver, *Bertram Grosvenor Goodhue*, 119.

19. Donald W. Curl, *Mizner's Florida: American Resort Architecture* (New York: The Architectural History Foundation, and Cambridge, Massachusetts, and London, England, The MIT Press, 1984), xi–xii, 1.

20. E. C. Pentland, "Santa Barbara and Its Beautiful Homes," *Los Angeles Times*, October 31, 1915.

21. "Is Reminiscent of Former Days. New Santa Barbara Mansion Planned on Spanish Lines," *Los Angeles Times* (July 14, 1918). Charles Over Cornelius, "The Residence of Major J. H. H. Peshine, Santa Barbara, California, Myron Hunt, Architect," *Architectural Record* 45, no. 2 (February 1919): 98–115. The house is located at 935 San Andres Street.

22. St. Saviour's Chapel originally was built at Sixteenth Street and St. Andrews Place on the Harvard campus. Winslow's participation is noted in "New Campus Structure, Chapel for Harvard Military School." *Los Angeles Times*, November 1, 1914. As Winslow had gone to California in 1911 to work on the Panama-California International Exposition in San Diego, it is tempting to speculate that the impetus to build in the Spanish style was his. In 1937 the chapel was cut into sixteen sections and moved to the school's new campus in North Hollywood. Susan Wells, *Harvard-Westlake: 100 Years* (Harvard-Westlake School: A Tehabi Book, 2002), 28–29. I thank Ann-Marie Whitman, Executive Assistant to the President, for opening the chapel to me on short notice.

23. "Country Houses of Southern California. Mr. Reginald D. Johnson Describes an Architecture in Harmony with the Matchless California Landscape, in an Interview with John Taylor Boyd, Jr.," *Arts & Decoration* 32, no. 5 (March 1930): 52, 98.

24. Winsor Soule, "Santa Barbara Architecture," *Architect and Engineer* 9, no. 3 (December 1924): 50–55.

25. Patricia Gebhard, *George Washington Smith: Architect of the Spanish Colonial Revival* (Salt Lake City: Gibbs Smith, Publisher, 2005). Information about Smith's contemporary work comes from entries Lutah Maria Riggs made on her 1922 desk calendar. She noted City Hall Plaza on May 3 and 4; the Lobero Theater on May 30; and the *Daily News* drawings on June 18. Architecture and Design Collection, University Art Museum, University of California, Santa Barbara.

CHAPTER 2
The Steedmans of St. Louis

1. "George Fox Steedman, " *Harvard College Class of 1892, Twenty-fifth Anniversary Report, 1892–1917* (Norwood, Massachusetts: Privately Printed for the Class by the Plimpton Press, 1917), 215.

2. "George Fox Steedman," *Harvard College Class of 1892, Thirtieth Anniversary Report, 1892–1922* (Norwood, Massachusetts: Privately Printed for the Class by the Plimpton Press, 1922), 239.

3. George Fox Steedman, Diary, 1892, Harvard University, Cambridge, Casa.

4. "Society," *St. Louis Globe-Democrat*, June 28, 1903. [News clipping, no title]. In Sprague Scrapbook, 6: 25, Missouri Historical Society Library. "Society," *St. Louis Post-Dispatch*, June 28, 1903.

5. "1892. Mary Institute, Graduation of the Twenty-sixth Class. June Third, at Half-Past Ten." Casa. "Graduates, 1892," *Mary Institute (Washington University). Thirty-third Year 1892–93* (St. Louis: Nixon-Jones Printing Co., 1893), 41. University Archives, Washington University, St. Louis.

6. "Mt. Lowe," *Los Angeles Times*, February 17, 1896. Kate Howard to Carrie Robb Howard, February 2, 12, 25, 28, [1896], Casa.

7. The European trips are similarly confirmed in correspondence from Kate Howard to Carrie Robb Howard, Casa.

8. Pierce P. Furber, local representative of the Boston firm Peabody & Stearns, designed the Howard house. Charles C. Savage, *Architecture of the Private Streets of St. Louis: The Architects and the Houses They Designed* (Columbia: University of Mis-

souri Press, 1987), 25. Although one historian characterized Vandeventer as "… too pretentiously exclusive for its own good," its early decline, beginning in the 1890s, resulted from encroaching commercial development. The eastern block was demolished between 1948 and 1950, the western in 1958. Savage, 22. Alexander Scott McConachie, "The 'Big Cinch': A Business Elite in the Life of a City, St. Louis, 1895–1915," (Ph.D. dissertation, Washington University, 1976), 327. Quoted in David T. Beito and Bruce Smith, "The Formation of Urban Infrastructure through Nongovernmental Planning: The Private Places of St. Louis, 1869–1920," *Journal of Urban History* 16, no. 3 (May 1990): 266. "Mrs. Howard Head of Club," *St. Louis Globe-Democrat*, November 11, 1913.

9. The St. Louis Social Register indicates that they lived with Carrie Steedman's mother at 33 Vandeventer between 1907 and 1910. Indenture, April 15, 1905, City of St. Louis Recorder of Deeds Archives Department.

10. Beito and Smith, "Formation," 267.

11. Savage, *Architecture*, 43.

12. Lawrence Mauran served as an usher for Steedman at his wedding. "Society," *St. Louis Post-Dispatch*, June 28, 1903. Photographs of the Steedman house appear in Julius K. Hunter, *Westmoreland and Portland Places: The History and Architecture of America's Premier Private Streets, 1888–1988* (Columbia: University of Missouri Press, 1988), 143, 202. A map on page 16 shows the location of the house and its relation to a house built in 1923 by Steedman's brother, Edmund, next door at number 32 and to a house at number 42 occupied briefly by the eldest Steedman brother, Harrison. A partial set of plans of the house at 34 Westmoreland was deposited at Casa del Herrero in 2007 by the Steedmans' grandson, Albert P. Hinckley, Jr.

13. The date the house was completed is inconclusive. Although records in the City of St. Louis Building Division indicate that the permit was issued March 9, 1909, the permit itself and all other records prior to 1940 have been discarded.

14. St. Louis City Directory, 1919.

15. William H. Smith, M.D., to Steedman, July 7, 1922, Casa.

16. "The James Harrison Steedman Memorial Fellowship in Architecture at Washington University, 1925," Casa. "James H. Steedman Fellowship Awarded," *St. Louis Daily Globe-Democrat*, April 3, 1927. "George F. Hellmuth, 92; founder of international architecture firm," *St. Louis Post-Dispatch*, November 7, 1999. William P. Wischmeyer, Washington University in St. Louis, to author, February 2, 2006.

17. "Agreement … November 9, 1928, by and between George Fox Steedman … and the Board of Directors of the Public Library of the City of St. Louis …." Steedman to Mr. [Arthur E.] Bostwick, October 14, 1926, both courtesy of the St. Louis Public Library.

18. [Bostwick] to Steedman, October 18, 1926, St. Louis Public Library. "George F. Steedman Presents $60,000 Gift to Library," *St. Louis Globe-Democrat*, November 23, 1928. "The Steedman Library Gift," *St. Louis Globe-Democrat*, November 24, 1928. "St. Louis Man Makes Gift to Architecture," *Christian Science Monitor*, November 27, 1928. "The Steedman Architectural Collection," *St. Louis Public Library Monthly Bulletin* New ser., 26, no. 12 (December 1928): 372. "Public Library Recipient of Valuable Collection of Books on Architecture," *St. Louisan* 3, no. 48 (December 1, 1928): 1. "Valuable Collection of Works on Architecture Donated to Public Library," *Know St. Louis Weekly* (December 2, 1928): 33, 39. "The Steedman Gift," *St. Louis Public Library Annual Report 1928–1929*, 49–51. "Steedman Memorial Room," *St. Louis Public Library Annual Report* 1930, 21–22, 46.

19. Information about Mullgardt's role is inconclusive. Although he frequently is cited as the designer, no substantiating evidence has been found to support the claim. Mullgardt was the younger brother of the much better known architect Louis Christian Mullgardt who is remembered for his work on the 1915 Panama-Pacific International Exhibition and the M. H. de Young Museum in San Francisco.

20. J. L. Mauran to Steedman, February 16, 1928, St. Louis Public Library.

21. Agreement, November 9, 1928. The drawings are in the collection of the Missouri Historical Society, St. Louis. "A Private-Public Library," *St. Louis Globe-Democrat Sunday Magazine*, December 16, 1934. Steedman to Merritt A. Vinson, March 10, 1937, Casa.

22. Steedman to Bostwick, October 22, 1926, Casa.

23. White to Steedman, September 11, 1931; February 13, 1934; Steedman Cardiac Fund, February 28, 1934; 1934 Casa Bank Accounts; White to Steedman, May 7, 1934, Casa. Frederick A. Washburn, M.D., *The Massachusetts General Hospital, Its Development, 1900–1935* (Boston: Houghton Mifflin Company and Cambridge, Massachusetts: The Riverside Press, 1939), 377–78; Louise Dattoli, Development Office, Massachusetts General Hospital, to author, September 21, 2006.

24. Steedman handwritten note, Casa.

25. "Miss K. Steedman Engaged to Marry," *New York Times*, May 17, 1928. "Steedman-Hinckley Wedding Late Today," *St. Louis Post-Dispatch*, June 14, 1928. "Social Items," *St. Louis Post-Dispatch*, June 14, 1928. "Society News," *St. Louis Star*, June 14, 1928. "Society News," *St. Louis Daily Globe-Democrat*, June 14, 1928. "Society News," *St. Louis Daily Globe-Democrat*, June 15, 1928. "Society News," *St. Louis Star*, June 15, 1928. "Steedman-Hinckley," *New York Times*, June 16, 1928. "Hinckley-Steedman," *New York Times*, June 17, 1928.

26. "Society News," *St. Louis Daily Globe-Democrat*, November 5, 1930. The engagement was announced in "Society News," *St. Louis Daily Globe-Democrat*, November 7, 1930 and "Medora Steedman to Wed George E. Bass," *St. Louis Post-Dispatch*, October 7, 1930. Additional accounts of the wedding were in the *St. Louis Daily Globe-Democrat*, November 2, 1930, and "Social Activities," *St. Louis Post-Dispatch*, November 4, 1930.

CHAPTER 3
Creating Casa del Herrero

1. Arthur Byne to Julia Morgan, December 15, 1921, Morgan Papers.

2. Dated photographs of the Steedman family taken at Mission San Juan Capistrano confirm a visit to California in 1919 but no additional documentation about this trip has been located. George, Carrie, and Medora arrived in Santa Barbara on January 12, 1921, and stayed at 47 (now 763) Ashley, which was owned by Philip S. and Effie Dowson. Jessie Mary Bryant, "Society," *Morning Press* (Santa Barbara), January 15, 1921. Harrison and Virginia Steedman were at number 41 (now 745). At the time, Dr. Sansum was based at the Potter Metabolic Clinic at Cottage Hospital. His famous clinic was founded in 1928. Erno S. Daniel, M.D., Sansum-Santa Barbara Medical Foundation Clinic, to author, November 18, 2005. Walter A. Tompkins, "William D. Sansum, M.D. America's Diabetes Expert," in *Santa Barbara History Makers*, edited by Barbara Hathaway Tompkins (Santa Barbara: McNally & Loftin, Publishers, 1983), 363–67. "Harrison Steedman Dies in California," *St. Louis Post-Dispatch*, July 2, 1921. "Steedman Funeral to be Held Wednesday," *St. Louis Post-Dispatch*, July 3, 1921. "Lieut. J. H. Steedman Dies in California," *St. Louis Globe-Democrat*, July 3, 1921. "Funeral for First St. Louisan in War," *St. Louis Globe-Democrat*, July 4, 1921.

3. The house was built for Mr. and Mrs. Harry Gantz; the drawings are now in the Prints and Photographs Division, Library of Congress, Washington, D.C. I thank Pamela Skewes-Cox, Craig's granddaughter, for this very welcome information.

4. Book 200, p. 351–52. 1922 Scott S. Durand to George F. Steedman, 6.86 acres.

5. "Local Mention," *The Ojai*, December 9, 1921. "Local Mention," *The Ojai*, March 17, 1922. "James O. Craig Architect, Dies," *Morning Press* (Santa Barbara), March 17, 1922. Standard Certificate of Death, State of California, Certification of Vital Record, County of Ventura, March 19, 1922.

6. "Winsor Soule," *Davis Commercial Encyclopedia of the Pacific Southwest. California, Nevada, Utah, Arizona* (Oakland, California: Ellis A. Davis, 1915), 345. Soule left Santa Barbara on February 16 and arrived back in New York on July 28, Ellis Island records. He returned to Santa Barbara on September 4, 1922. "Winsor Soule, Noted Local Architect, Back from Spain," *Morning Press* (Santa Barbara), September 6, 1922.

7. "Winsor Soule Will Tell of 4000 Mile Trip Through Spain," *Morning Press* (Santa Barbara), December 3, 1922. "Soule Will Tell of Spain and Show Pictures of Its Architectural Treasures," *Morning Press* (Santa Barbara), November 29, 1922. "Soule Lecture Intended As Aid to Home Builders," *Morning Press* (Santa Barbara), December 5, 1922. "Spain Revealed to Community Arts as Architect Sees It," *Morning Press* (Santa Barbara), December 6, 1922. The book, with an introduction by Ralph Adams Cram, was published by Architectural Book Pub-

lishing Co., Paul Wenzel and Maurice Krakow, New York, 1924.

8. Mary P. Bushnell Hazard and Caroline Hazard, widow and sister of Rowland Gibson Hazard, conceived the project. "Dedication of the Hazard Memorial," *Journal of the Museum of Comparative Oology* 2, nos. 3 and 4 (October 26, 1922): 1. The Hazards were members of a prominent Rhode Island family who had built winter houses behind the mission; Caroline Hazard was president of Wellesley College for many years and donated the land for the memorial. I thank Lisa Rowlison and Terry Sheridan, Santa Barbara Museum of Natural History, and Mother Maria, St. Mary's Retreat House, for their help.

9. Information on Brewster's arrival in Smith's office comes from a note on Lutah Maria Riggs's 1923 desk calendar, Architecture and Design Collection, University Art Museum, University of California, Santa Barbara.

10. Steven Timbrook, "Ralph Tallant Stevens, A Legacy of Landscapes," *Lotusland Newsletter for Members*, 8, no. 4 (Winter 1999): 1–2. "Spotlight on Ralph Tallant Stevens," *Newsletter of the Casa del Herrero* (Summer 2003): 1. Sharon Crawford, "Lotusland—Before Madame Ganna Walska." In *Ganna Walska, Lotusland, The Garden and Its Creators* (Santa Barbara: Produced for Ganna Walska Lotusland Foundation by Companion Press, 1996), 23–27. Deanna Hatch, Lotusland, to author, December 30, 2005.

11. Mary Louise Days, "City Park Superintendents," in *Park Histories* (Santa Barbara: City of Santa Barbara, June 1977), 6.

12. Steedman to Smith, March 7, 1923.

13. Architecture and Design Collection, University Art Museum, University of California, Santa Barbara.

14. Stevens to Steedman, November 20, 1922, Casa.

15. Note on Scheme B, Casa.

16. Notes on Scheme C, Casa.

17. This note is written in Steedman's hand on an undated drawing, UCSB.

18. The trip occurred between December 1922 and early January 1923. Lutah Maria Riggs notes on her calendar, Architecture and Design Collection, University Art Museum, University of California, Santa Barbara.

19. Steedman to Smith, March 7, 1923.

20. Smith to Steedman, July 12, 1923; December 4, 1923. Stevens to Steedman, December 6, 1923, Casa. Hartfeld was Dutch and according to his son, Edward, had made his way to America "in steerage." He worked between 1916 and 1918 on the grounds of the new E. W. Marland estate in Ponca City, Oklahoma, before moving to Santa Barbara. Edward A. Hartfeld, "The Greening of Santa Barbara," *Noticias*, Quarterly Magazine of the Santa Barbara Historical Society, 47, no. 4 (Winter 2001): 83; Edward A. Hartfeld to author, January 5, 2006. Darlene Platt, Operations Assistant, Marland's Grand Home, to author, February 3, 2006.

21. Steedman to Smith, March 7, March 9, 1923.

22. Louis La Beaume and William Booth Papin, *The Picturesque Architecture of Mexico* (New York: Architectural Book Publishing Company, 1915).

23. Mildred Stapley Byne to Julia Morgan, October 1, 1921, Morgan Papers.

24. La Beaume, "A Little Tour in Spain," *Journal of the American Institute of Architects*, 13, no. 3 (March 1925): 82.

25. Steedman's handwritten notes, Casa.

26. La Beaume, "A Little Tour in Spain," 12, no. 11 (November 1924): 459–60. After his trip in 1922 Winsor Soule noted the great popularity of American cars in Spain and added that Henry Ford had an assembly plant in Bordeaux. "Winsor Soule, Noted Local Architect, Back from Spain," *Morning Press* (Santa Barbara), September 6, 1922.

27. La Beaume, "A Little Tour in Spain," 465–66.

28. Ibid., 364.

29. Steedman to Smith, June 17, 1923.

30. Byne to Smith, September 10, 1923.

31. Byne to Steedman, September 12, 24, 1923. Both Casa.

32. Byne to Smith, July 6, 1923.

33. Steedman to Smith, July 18, 1923.

34. Steedman to Smith, n.d., but after July 20, 1923. Byne to Steedman, September 12, 1923, Casa.

35. Steedman to Smith, July 16, 1923.

36. Smith to Steedman, July 23, August 7, 1923. Steedman to Smith, August 24, 1923. Byne to Smith, September 10, 1923. Byne to Steedman, September 12, 1923, Casa.

37. Steedman to Smith, November 5, 30, 1923.

38. Byne to Smith, July 6, 1923. Smith to Wheeler, Elder & Elder, August 7, 1923.

39. Smith to Steedman, October 12, 1923. Smith to Byne, November 15, 1923.

40. Steedman to Wheeler, Elder & Elder, October 13, 1923. Byne to Steedman, November 6, 1923. Steedman to Smith, October 8, 1923.

41. Steedman to Smith, November 5; November 30; December 5, 1923. Smith to Steedman, December 27, 1923.

42. Byne to Steedman, ca. October 1923 (not in archives; mentioned in Steedman to Smith, October 29, 1923). Smith to Steedman, December 4, 1923. Steedman to Byne, December 11, 1923.

43. M. S. Byne to Steedman, January 9, 1924.

44. Byne to Steedman, January 14, 1924.

45. Byne to Stedman, January 21, 1924.

46. Steedman to Smith, January 3, 1924. Steedman to Stevens, November 14, 1923, Casa. Steedman to Smith, December 14, 1923.

47. Smith to Steedman, January 11, 1924. Steedman to Smith, January 14, 1924.

48. Steedman to Smith, February 8, 1924; March 2, 1925. The new University Club building opened July 7, 1922. It was published in *Architectural Digest* (Southern California Business Edition) (1923): 4–8. An advertisement for B. B. Bell appears on page 63; another for Marshall Laird is on page 66. Laird's most visible work in Santa Barbara is the tympanum on the Anapamu facade of the public library, carved from a design by Carleton Winslow. Its symbolic importance was sadly diminished when the entrance to the library was relocated during a remodeling and expansion completed in 1980. Piri Korngold Nesselrod, *Biography of a Library* (Santa Barbara: n.p., 1990): 28. "Looking through the Lens at Bits of Life," *Los Angeles Times*, March 14, 1924.

49. Dean Smith, "Castle Hot Springs: Remote Resort for the Rich and Famous." *Arizona Trend* (January 1987): 81–82, 84. "Hot Springs Still Bubble with Charm," *Arizona Republic*, October 7, 1990. Debbie Newman, Librarian, Arizona Historical Society, to author, October 19, 2005. Steedman to Smith, March 10, 1924 (two letters).

50. Smith to Steedman, March 19, April 15, 1924.

51. Smith to Steedman, April 21, 1924. Steedman to Smith, May 2, 1924.

52. Smith to Steedman, May 23, 1924. William L. Snook and Oades John Kenyon formed a partnership in 1916 and went on to distinguish themselves as builders of several of Santa Barbara's finest public buildings, including El Paseo and the Lobero Theatre, and many houses designed by Smith. Michael James Phillips, "William L. Snook" and "O. J. Kenyon," in *History of Santa Barbara County California. From Its Earliest Settlement to the Present Time.* Volume I (Chicago, San Francisco, and Los Angeles: The S. J. Clarke Publishing Co., 1927), 398–99, 436–37. "William Snook, Local Builder, Dies at 79," *Santa Barbara News Press*, December 1, 1955. "Funeral Planned for Contractor," *Los Angeles Times*, December 3, 1955.

53. Steedman to Smith, June 4, 1924. Smith to Steedman, May 31, 1924; June 4, 1924. Steedman to Smith, June 7, 1924.

54. Smith to Steedman, June 9, 1924. Steedman to Smith, June 19, 1924. The estimate has not been located in the Casa archives.

55. Steedman to Smith, January 14, June 23, June 28, 1924.

56. Steedman to Smith, July 8, 1924.

57. Smith to Steedman, July 25, 1924. Wire, Smith to Steedman, August 15, 1924. Steedman to Smith, August 15, 1924. Smith to Miss Meyers, August 16, 1924. Smith to Steedman, August 16, 1924.

58. Steedman to Smith, August 24, 1924. Smith to Steedman, September 27, 1924.

59. Steedman to Smith, September 12, 14, 1924.

60. Steedman to Smith, August 15, 1924. Brewster to Steedman, October 21; December 29, 1924. Steedman to Brewster, January 14, 1925.

61. Brewster to Steedman, January 28, 1925. Steedman to Smith, February 5, 1925. Smith to Steedman, February 9, 1925.

62. Steedman to Smith, Sunday evening [February 15, 1925]; Thursday P.M. [March 5, 1925].

63. Steedman to Smith, April 1, 1925.

64. Smith to Steedman, May 29, 1925. Steedman to Smith, June 3, 1925.

65. Smith to Steedman, May 29, 1925. The Santa Barbara Club was organized in 1892 for the purpose of providing a comfortable meeting place for local ranchers and affluent easterners living and vacationing in Santa Barbara and by the mid twenties included Dwight Murphy, George Washington Smith, Winsor Soule, and Francis T. Underhill among its members. The building, designed by Francis Wilson, who also was responsible

for the public library, was completed in 1904. Edward S. Spaulding, *Santa Barbara Club: A History* (Santa Barbara: Press of the Schauer Printing Studio, 1954). I thank the Santa Barbara Club for its cooperation.

66. Carrie, Katherine and Medora arrived July 3. Jessie Mary Bryant, "The Daily Round of Society," *Morning Press* (Santa Barbara), July 5, 1925.

CHAPTER 4
Playing Some More

1. Steedman to Smith, September 28, 1925.
2. Smith to Steedman, October 26; November 21, 1925. Steedman to Smith, November 30, 1925.
3. Steedman to Smith, September 30, 1925.
4. Invoice, Byne to Steedman, January 14, 1928, with "voucher 17" noted in Steedman's hand, Casa. The south elevation was published in "The California Homes of George Washington Smith," *Pacific Coast Architect* 29, no. 5 (May 1926): 11. Views of the living room appeared in *American Country Houses of Today*, 1927, with a Preface by Alfred Hopkins (New York: Architectural Book Publishing Company, Inc., Paul Wenzel, and Maurice Krakow, 1926): 124.
5. Steedman to Smith, June 19, 1924. Steedman to Stevens, June 23, 1924.
6. "Plant Expert Peter Riedel Dies," *Santa Barbara News Press*, December 6, 1954. Virginia Padilla, "Peter Riedel," in *Southern California Gardens: An Illustrated History* (Berkeley and Los Angeles: University of California Press, 1961), 186–91. I thank Kathryn Smith for bringing this book to my attention. Riedel advertised regularly in *Santa Barbara Gardener* and trumpeted his accomplishments in 1930: "The book Glimpses of Santa Barbara and Montecito Gardens, by Mrs. Bissell, contains 33 pictures of local gardens. Fourteen of them are of gardens built by P. Riedel." *Santa Barbara Gardener* 5, no. 11 (October 1930): 8. The same advertisement appeared in November and December 1930 and in January and February 1931. A slightly revised version appeared in March and April 1931.
7. Steedman to Smith, June 3, 1925.
8. Note on Steedman Scheme C, Casa.
9. Deed, John Whittemore to G. F. Steedman, more of Cota Tract with stipulations on structures and tree height. Official Records, Book 69, pp. 415–18. Filed September 28, 1925.
10. Steedman to Smith, September 28, 30, 1925.
11. David Streatfield, "Underhill, Francis Townsend," in Charles A. Birnbaum and Julie K. Fix, *Pioneers of American landscape Design II: An Annotated Bibliography* (Washington, D.C.: U.S. Department of the Interior National Park Service Cultural Resources Heritage Preservation Services Historic Landscape Initiative, 1995), 143–45. "Portfolio of Current Architecture," *Architectural Record* 45, no. 1 (January 1919): 65–70. Underhill's obituary describes him as a "clubman, architect, horse fancier, yachts man, cattle breeder, world traveler and raconteur." "Francis T. Underhill Dead," *Los Angeles Times*, August 11, 1929.
12. [No title], *Morning Press* (Santa Barbara),

November 26, 1919. William Frederick Peters, "Lockwood de Forest, Landscape Architect: Santa Barbara, California, 1896–1949," 11. Michael Redmon, "History 101," *Santa Barbara Independent*, February 22–29, 1996. Ellis Island records.

13. The drawing is in the Lockwood de Forest Collection (1965-2), Environmental Design Archives, University of California, Berkeley.
14. Casa archives.
15. Edward H. Hart to author, October 17, 2005; May 22, 2007. A list of building costs compiled by Steedman in 1928 includes the annotation: "This covers … Alterations … North court…," indicating that the work was complete at that time, Casa.
16. Steedman, "Notes re tile for star pool shown on sketch #2," June 2, 1928, Casa.
17. Steedman to James R. H. Wagner, June 9, 1927; J. R. Whittemore to Steedman, June 12, 1927; Steedman to Whittemore, June 17, 1927, all Casa.
18. "Death Claims J. J. Plunkett," *Santa Barbara News Press*, May 29, 1946. "Funeral Rites To Be Held Friday for 'Joe' Plunkett," *Santa Barbara News Press*, May 30, 1946.
19. Standard Form of Agreement between Owner and Architect; H. W. Howell to Steedman, October 1, 1928, both Casa.
20. Invoices, John Hartfeld, Thompson & Banks, Edwards, Plunkett & Howell, Casa.
21. The certificate, dated February 1930, is in the Casa archives. "Honor Awards: Civic and Commercial Architecture in Santa Barbara and Montecito in the Years 1928–1929. Arranged by the Plans Committee of the Community Arts Association." Copy in scrapbook, CDCC Community Arts Association—Plans & Planting, 1923–1931, Special Collections, University of California, Santa Barbara. "Santa Barbara Awards," *Architect and Engineer* 101, no. 1 (April 1930): 110. Steedman to Chase, March 1, 1930. Harold Chase Papers, Special Collections, University of California, Santa Barbara. I thank Pamela Skewes-Cox for apprising me of this letter.
22. Elaine Griscom, Santa Barbara Regional Oral History Clearinghouse. Santa Barbara Historical Museum. *Joe Acquistapace*. January 14, 1984, 27.
23. Steedman to Wheeler, Elder & Elder, December 12, 1923. "Tiles Bought by G. F. Steedman in Spain, in May and June, 1923," n.d., Casa.
24. Byne to Steedman, January 20, 21, 1924.
25. Steedman to Smith, July 16, 1923.
26. Steedman to Chemla, June 9, 1927, Casa.
27. Steedman to Byne, June 2, 1928, Casa.
28. Re Sketch #4 for Garage Floor and Dado, June 2, 1928, Casa.
29. Riggs to Steedman, February 26, 1931, Casa.
30. Permit No. 181, County of Santa Barbara, June 8, 1933. This is the earliest permit on record for work at the Casa. It is held today in the Architectural Archives, American Institute of Architects, Santa Barbara Chapter. Ernst Kloss, *Speculum Humanae Salvationis; Ein Niederländisches Blockbuch* (Munich, Germany: München R. Piper & Co., 1925), Casa.
31. Brewster to Steedman, October 31, 1933; Steedman to Brewster, October 26, 1933; Brewster to Steedman, October 28, 1933,

all Casa.

32. Permit No. 203, June 26, 1934, Architectural Archives, American Institute of Architects, Santa Barbara Chapter. Ted [Edwin Steedman] to Steedman, September 17, 1934, Casa.
33. Arthur Byne and Mildred Stapley, *Provincial Houses in Spain* (New York: William Helburn Inc., 1925), i.

CHAPTER 5
Life in the Casa

1. Steedman to Mitchell D. Follansbee, Esq., January 21, 1937, Casa
2. In 1930 a St. Louis society columnist noted: "Miss [Medora] Steedman has been away from St. Louis much of the time, spending several months out of the year with her parents at their handsome home in Santa Barbara." "Society News," *St. Louis Daily Globe-Democrat*, October 7, 1930.
3. Steedman to Byne, June 10, 1924.
4. Jessie Mary Bryant, "The Daily Round of Society," *Morning Press* (Santa Barbara) July 19, 1925.
5. "George Fox Steedman," *Harvard College Class of 1892, Report XI, 1892–1928* (Norwood, Massachusetts: Privately Printed for the Class), 194.
6. Steedman to Harold D. Jacobs, *Morning Press* (Santa Barbara), May 28, 1936, Casa. "Society Page," *Morning Press* (Santa Barbara), April 10, 1928. Juana Neal Levy, "Society; Affairs of the Week," *Los Angeles Times*, April 15, 1928. A. Scott Berg, *Lindbergh* (New York: G. P. Putnam's Sons, 1998), 95–96, 109, 163–65.
7. The 1925 tours took place April 20–22. They were organized by the Plans and Planting Committee of the Community Arts Association and the Little Gardens Club with the goal of awakening "… a desire in every citizen of the city to beautify his or her place this spring." "Prize Gardens of City Open to Inspection," *Morning Press* (Santa Barbara), April 12, 1925. "100 Garden Tags Issued," *Morning Press* (Santa Barbara), April 17, 1925. "The Daily Round of Society," *Morning Press* (Santa Barbara), April 19, 1925.
8. "Garden Club Special Train Will Reach City Tonight and Delegates Open Meet Tuesday," *Daily News* (Santa Barbara), April 12, 1926. "Special Train Brings Garden Club Hosts," *Morning Press* (Santa Barbara), April 13, 1926. "Special Train Brings Garden Club Members," *Daily News* (Santa Barbara), April 13, 1926. Bulletin of *The Garden Club of America* No. 9 (Third Series), (May 1926): 2–3, 7, 12–13, 18–19.
9. Minutes, Garden Club of Santa Barbara, January 21, 1929: 4.
10. "Steedman, Mrs. G. F. Valley Road, Montecito," is listed as a member in *The Garden Club of Santa Barbara and Montecito California 1926*. "Wild Life Poster Wins Medal," *Los Angeles Times*, March 6, 1935.
11. "George Fox Steedman," *Harvard College Class of 1892, Report XI, 1892–1928* (Norwood, Massachusetts: Privately Printed for the Class), 193–94.
12. Wagner to Steedman, April 2, 1927, Casa.
13. Wagner to Steedman, May 2, 1927, Casa.
14. Wagner to Steedman, May 2, 1927, October 1, 1930; both Casa. Official Records Book 224, p. 69, 1930.

15. Wagner to Steedman, October 4, 1928; May 29, 1928; July 14, 1928; August 23, 1928; October 4, 1928; March 28, 1933; November 18, 1933; July 20, 1934; June 18, 1935; October 15, 1935; December 14, 1935; January 21, 1936; all Casa.

16. Steedman to Sam J. Stanwood, June 8, 1931, Casa, contributions folder, file 2. "New Life for Horse Show Sure," *Los Angeles Times,* June 19, 1931.

17. "Horse Show 'Second Nighters' Get Thrills of Old West Life," *Morning Press* (Santa Barbara), July 25, 1931. "Horses Thrill Large Throng," *Los Angeles Times,* July 26, 1931. In fact, attending the races in Los Angeles was a favorite pastime. "G. F. Steedmans View Races." *Morning Press* (Santa Barbara), February 24, 1936. According to Carrie Steedman's grandson, Albert Hinckley, she often went to Santa Anita with her friend Amy Du Pont. One of their chauffeurs would drive them to the Santa Barbara airport for the flight to Los Angeles; the other's chauffeur, who had driven ahead, would meet them and drive them to Arcadia. Albert Hinckley to author, July 17, 2008.

18. "Fleischmann Heads Museum," *Daily News* (Santa Barbara), January 17, 1934. "Fleischmann Heads Museum Directorate," *Morning Press* (Santa Barbara), January 17, 1934. "Garden Club Flower Show at Museum of Natural History Attracts Many Visitors," *Daily News* (Santa Barbara) March 16, 1934. "Mrs. George Steedman Takes Top Honors in Annual Flower Exhibit," *Morning Press* (Santa Barbara), March 16, 1934. "Garden Club Will Assist Federation," *Daily News* (Santa Barbara) September 12, 1934.

19. "George Fox Steedman," *Harvard College Class of 1892, Report XII, 1892–1932* (Norwood, Massachusetts: Privately Printed for the Class by the Plimpton Press), 198.

20. Steedman to Paul Dudley White, December 30, 1936, Casa.

21. George F. Steedman, "Herraro [*sic*], The 'Lost Wax' Process of Metal Casting," MS, March 1938, Casa.

22. For a general discussion of patent furniture, which often incorporated adjustable mechanical apparatus, see Rodris Roth, "Nineteenth-Century American Patent Furniture," in David A. Hanks, *Innovative Furniture in America From 1800 to the Present* (New York: Horizon Press, 1981), 23–46.

23. Steedman's comments about wine are in a notebook now in the shop office. Masson to Steedman, November 17, 1931; September 8, 1932, Casa.

24. Steedman to Berkeley Yeast Laboratory, August 26, 1936; Steedman to Masson, August 6, 1936; October 3, 1935; January 21, 1936, all Casa.

25. Typewritten statement in donations file, Casa.

26. Roxanne Grant Lapidus, "Brothers in Art," *Noticias,* Quarterly Magazine of the Santa Barbara Historical Society, 49, no. 3 (Autumn 2003): 73–74.

27. Channing Peake, interview by Cynthia Haskell, May 12, 1985, tape 1, side 1, Santa Barbara Museum of Art. I thank Heather Broadhead for her help.

28. Gordon Grant file, Casa.

29. "Duralumin," *Encyclopaedia Britannica.* 2007. Encyclopaedia Britannica Online, 7.

30. "Art and Artists," *Morning Press* (Santa Barbara), ca. February 1936.

31. Edward Alden Jewell, "64 Artists Offer Rome Prix Entries," *New York Times,* May 15, 1935. Arthur Millier, "Beach Exhibits Studied as Vote Scrap Brews," *Los Angeles Times,* August 7, 1938.

32. Author to F. M. Richards Library, Brady Texas, January 18, 2006. Ed Stevenson, Postmaster, Brady, Texas, to author, January 24, 2006. Ann Shuffler, Richards Memorial Library, to author, January 25, 2006. Philip Parisi, *The Texas Post Office Murals: Art of the People* (College Station, Texas: Texas A & M University Press, 2004), 4–5, 28. Lapidus, "Brothers …," 77–78. Other murals by Grant have fared less well. One, at the Alhambra, California, post office (1938) has been painted over. Another at John Marshall High School in Los Angeles has disappeared. It is poorly documented and may not have been part of the Section of Fine Arts program. Joanna Erdos, John Marshall High School, to author, January 18, 2006.

33. Edward H. Hart to author, October 17, 2005. The Hart family left sometime in mid 1931; Joseph R. Legg and his wife were living in the butler's cottage by August 1. Invoice, Mission Oak Nursery, August 1, 1931, approved by J. R. Legg, Casa.

34. The drawings are dated September 28 and October 4, 1930, Casa.

35. Edward A. Hartfeld, "The Greening of Santa Barbara," *Noticias,* Quarterly Magazine of the Santa Barbara Historical Society, 47, no. 4 (Winter 2001): 83. Joe Acquistapace, interview by Elaine Griscom, January 14, 1984, Santa Barbara Regional Oral History Clearinghouse. Santa Barbara Historical Museum, 2, 9. 68. Cancelled checks, Casa. 1934 Santa Barbara City Directory. Clarence Baker, who was hired as chauffeur in 1932, and his family were living in the gardener's cottage.

36. Acquistapace, ibid., 12, 19, 20.

37. *Modern Gardening* 1, no. 2 (February 28, 1938): 2. "Here and there with the Rambler." *Modern Gardening* 2, no. 1 (March 2, 1940): 4. Acquistapace's activities also were mentioned in the September 1, 1939, and August 1, 1940, issues.

38. Victoria Padilla, *Southern California Gardens* (Berkeley and Los Angeles: University of California Press, 1961), 107.

39. Ibid., 200. Orpet invoices, Casa.

40. "Memories of Casa del Herrero – Margaret Hinckley Wise – October 1999," typescript, Casa. Quoted with permission.

CHAPTER 6
A Good, Satisfying Home

1. Steedman to Smith, June 10, 1924.

2. Arthur Byne and Mildred Stapley made the point in 1925: "To the popular notion Andalusia is all Spain and Andalusian architecture is Spanish architecture. This widespread misapprehension is due to the fact that it was the picturesque semi-Moorish stucco buildings of Andalusia which were carried to the New World and later accepted throughout both Americas as the one typical style of the mother country." *Provincial Houses in Spain* (New York: William Helburn Inc., 1925), i.

3. Smith to Byne, July 26, 1923. A. Lawrence Kocher, "The Country House. Are We Developing an American Style?" *Architectural Record* 60, no. 5 (November 1926): 388, 389–90.

4. Gebhard, *Smith,* 3. Steedman to Smith, July 16, 1923.

5. Smith to Byne, July 26, 1923. Steedman to Smith, June 13, 1924. Smith to Byne, July 30, 1924.

6. Austin Whittlesey, *The Minor Ecclesiastical Domestic and Garden Architecture of Southern Spain* (New York: Architectural Book Publishing Co., 1917). Steedman to Smith, June 30, [1924]. William Lawrence Bottomley, *Spanish Details* (New York: William Helburn Inc., 1924). The book is dedicated to Mildred Stapley Byne. Rose Standish Nichols, *Spanish & Portuguese Gardens* (Boston and New York: Houghton Mifflin Company, and Cambridge, Massachusetts: The Riverside Press, 1924). The Bynes' articles were collected and published as *Spanish Gardens and Patios* (Philadelphia & London: J. B. Lippincott Company, and New York: *Architectural Record,* 1924).

7. Guy Lowell, *Smaller Italian Villas & Farmhouses* (New York: The Architectural Book Publishing Co., 1916).

8. Byne to Steedman, June 8, 1927, Casa.

9. Albert Hinckley to author, January 24, 2006.

10. Steedman, "Inventory – Spanish Purchases – 1923 & 1924," Casa.

11. Arthur Byne, "Old Spanish Furniture," *Good Furniture* 4, no. 6 (March 1915): 338–42.

12. Mildred Stapley Byne, "The Peak of Spain's Decorative Art," *Arts and Decoration* 28, no. 5 (March 1928): 48–49. Arthur Byne and Mildred Stapley, *Spanish Interiors and Furniture* (New York: William Helburn Inc., 1922), v.

13. Byne and Stapley, *Spanish Interiors and Furniture,* v.

14. Ibid., iii.

15. Mildred Stapley Byne to Julia Morgan, October 1, 1921; [Morgan] to Byne, Stapley, September 19, 1921; Morgan to Stapley, November 1, 1921; Morgan to Mr. and Mrs. Arthur Stapley Byne, November 18, 1921; Morgan to Byne, February 24, 1925, all Morgan Papers.

16. Byne to Steedman, July 1, 1923, Casa. Steedman to Smith, November 9, 1923.

17. There were additional shipments for which surviving documentation is incomplete.

18. Byne to Steedman, September 12, 1923, Casa. Steedman to Smith, October 8, 1923. Steedman, "Inventory – Spanish Purchases – 1923 & 1924," Casa.

19. [Floyd Brewster] to Steedman, October 28, 1924. Steedman to Brewster, November 1, 1924. Smith to Steedman, June 30, 1926. As noted previously in the text, the panels were painted later by Channing Peake.

20. Mildred Stapley Byne, "Gothic Painted Ceilings from Teruel," *Art Bulletin* 9, no. 4 (June 1927): 341–51. For reproductions of the Teurel Cathedral ceiling, see José F. Ràfols, *Techumbres y Artesonados Espanoles* (Barcelona: Editorial Labor, 1926), front., pls. xl, xli.

21. Wire, Julia Morgan to Mildred Stapley, March 11, 1925, Morgan Papers. "Flem-

ish Tapestry Sells for $20,000," *New York Times*, January 16, 1927. The Taylor ceiling is discussed and illustrated in Felix Brun Gabarda, "La Techumbre de Villa Schifanoia," in *Artesonados Mudéjares de Teruel en el Extranjero* (Teruel: 2003), 89–139; in Mildred Stapley Byne and Arthur Byne, *Important Mediaeval and Early Renaissance Works of Art from Spain: Sculptures, Furniture, Textiles, Tapestries, and Rugs. Collection of Conde de las Almenas, Madrid, Spain* (New York: American Art Association, Inc., 1927), 292–94; and in Byne, "Gothic Painted Ceilings from Teruel," 341–51.

22. Byne and Stapley, *Spanish Interiors and Furniture*, iii; Steedman to Smith, June 17, 1923; September 14, 1924.

23. Mildred Stapley Byne, "The Peak of Spain's Decorative Art, Part Two," *Arts and Decoration* 28, no. 6 (April 1928): 48–49, 92. Byne to Steedman, September 12, 1923; September 24, 1923.

24. Byne and Stapley, *Spanish Interiors and Furniture*, vi.

25. Ibid., v.

26. Ibid., vii.

27. Marshall Laird to Smith, January 8, 1925; Laird to Steedman, March 12, 1925; Laird statements, n.d., all Casa.

28. Steedman to St. Louis Art Museum, December 24, 1923, Casa. Phyllis Ackerman, "The Atelier of Maitre Philippe," *Bulletin of the City Art Museum of St. Louis* 9, no 4 (October 1924): 54–57. The Steedmans' tapestry that was exhibited is approximately two-thirds its original size, the lower portion having been cut off at some point.

29. Valerie Rudy-Valli, Assistant Registrar, St. Louis Art Museum, to author, August 18, 2006. La Beaume to Steedman, November 30, 1925, Casa. "Paintings by Byne Are Exhibited Here," *St. Louis Daily Globe-Democrat*, November 18, 1925.

30. Mildred Stapley Byne and Arthur Byne. *Important Mediaeval and Early Renaissance Works of Art from Spain*. [11].

31. Byne to Julia Morgan, March 25, 1926, Morgan Papers.

32. Mildred Stapley, "Old Spanish Pottery" *The House Beautiful* 36 (September 1914): 126–28.

33. Arthur Byne, "Old Spanish Furniture" *Good Furniture* 4, no. 6 (March 1915): 338–42.

34. Mildred Stapley Byne, *Forgotten Shrines of Spain* (Philadelphia and London: J. B. Lippincott Company, 1926), 28.

35. Stapley to Morgan, October 1, 1921; Byne to Morgan, December 15, 1921, both Morgan Papers.

36. Byne to Steedman, December 2, 1926, Casa. Wire, Julia Morgan to Stapley, March 11, 1925, Morgan Papers. Byne, *Important Mediaeval and Early Renaissance Works of Art from Spain*, [11].

37. Byne, *Important Mediaeval and Early Renaissance Works of Art from Spain*, 192– [93].

38. Byne to Steedman, September 14, 1927, Casa.

39. Byne to Steedman, September 15, 1928; April 24, 1929, both Casa.

40. Byne to Steedman, May 4, 1930, Casa. Byne and Stapley, *Spanish Interiors and Furniture*, v.

41. Byne and Stapley, *Spanish Interiors and Furniture*, i, iii.

42. Steedman to Smith, April 15, 1925.

43. Byne to Steedman, May 4; March 24, 1930, both Casa.

44. Steedman to Stapley, September 10, 1935, Casa. "Arthur Byne Dies in Spain," *New York Times*, July 17, 1935. "Arthur Byne," *Revista Espanola de Arte* 4, no. 6 (July 1935): 295. "Deaths," *American Architect* 147, no. 2636 (August 1935): 106. "The Late Arthur Byne," *Apollo* 22 (September 1935): 179.

CHAPTER 7
Change

1. George Bass statement, December 2, 2003, Casa.

2. "Explosion Injuries Fatal to Gordon Kenneth Grant, Noted Artist," *Santa Barbara News Press*, March 2, 1940. "Cannon Kills Young Artist," *Los Angeles Times*, March 3, 1940. "Gordon K. Grant Killed," *New York Times*, March 3, 1940. "Inquest Dropped in Grant Death," *Santa Barbara News Press*, March 3, 1940. Final Services Are Held for Gordon Kenneth Grant." *Santa Barbara News Press*, March 4, 1940. "Death by Cannon Termed Accident," *Los Angeles Times*, March 4, 1940.

3. "G. F. Steedman, Fellowship Fund Donor, Dies at 69," *St. Louis Post-Dispatch*, April 29, 1940. "Geo. F. Steedman Dies in West," *St. Louis Daily Globe-Democrat*, April 30, 1940. "Geo. F. Steedman, Former St. Louis Man, Dies in West," *St. Louis Star-Times*, April 30, 1940. "George F. Steedman Will Be Buried in St. Louis," *St. Louis Star Times*, April 30, 1940. "Funeral at Cemetery for George F. Steedman," *St. Louis Post-Dispatch*, April 30, 1940.

4. Permit 2608, July 8, 1957. Architectural Archives, American Institute of Architects, Santa Barbara Chapter.

5. George Bass statement, December 2, 2003, Casa. Acquistapace was listed as a farmer in the 1944 Santa Barbara City Directory.

6. Last Will and Testament of George Fox Steedman, March 12, 1936. Included in Guaranty Trust Company of New York vs. Carrie H. Steedman, et al. Supreme Court, New York County, No. 26579 – 1941. Action to Settle Account of Trustee, Casa. I thank Bruce Glesby for clarifying this document.

7. George Bass interview, December 2, 2003. "George Bass of Montecito dies at age 82." *Santa Barbara News Press*, July 29, 1988, B-3.

8. History Meeting on the Steedman house. Mrs. Bass, Henzell, Gen. Muller in attendance. January 25, 1986. Tape recording in possession of Montecito History Committee Archives.

9. Medora Bass to Friend, October 13, 1986, Casa. "Bass to Donate Historic Estate to Community," *Montecito Life*, November 13, 1986.

10. Joan Jackson and Dan Eidelson to author, October 4, 2006. Jean Smith Goodrich to author, September 11, 2007.

11. Author-activist Medora Bass, 78, Dies," *Santa Barbara News Press*, December 7, 1987.

12. Heron Marquez Estrada, "Multimillion-dollar Estate Is Bequeathed to SBCC," *Santa Barbara News Press*, January 10, 1988.

13. George's sister Medora Bass also con-

tributed to the endowment.

14. David Bisol to author, June 22, 2007.

15. Edward A. Hartfeld to author, January 5, 2006.

16 Office of the Secretary, U. S. Department of the Interior. News Release. January 16, 2009. "Interior Secretary Kempthorne Designates 9 National Historic Landmarks in 9 States." www.doi.gov. National Historic Landmark Nomination: Steedman Estate /Casa del Herrero. February 25, 2009. http://www.nps.gov/history/nhl/Fall08 Nominaions/Casa%20del%20Herrero.pdf.

BIBLIOGRAPHY

1903

PERIODICALS

"Society." *St. Louis Post-Dispatch*, June 28, 1903.
Steedman/Howard wedding.

"Society." *St. Louis Daily Globe-Democrat*, June 28, 1903.
Steedman/Howard wedding.

1915

BOOKS

"George F. Steedman." In *Builders of American Business*. Chicago, New York, and London: A. W. Shaw Company, 1915, n.p.

1917

BOOKS

"George Fox Steedman." In *Harvard College Class of 1892, Twenty-fifth Anniversary Report, 1892–1917*. Norwood, Massachusetts: Privately Printed for the Class by the Plimpton Press, 215.

1922

BOOKS

"George Fox Steedman." In *Harvard College Class of 1892, Thirtieth Anniversary Report, 1892–1922*. Norwood, Massachusetts: Privately Printed for the Class by the Plimpton Press, 1922, 238–39.

1923

PERIODICALS

"Mrs. Kate M. Howard to be Buried Tuesday." *St. Louis Daily Globe-Democrat*, February 24, 1923.

1925

PERIODICALS

Bryant, Jessie Mary. "The Daily Round of Society." *Morning Press* (Santa Barbara), July 5, 1925.
Carrie, Katherine and Medora arrived in Santa Barbara Friday, July 3.

———. "The Daily Round of Society." *Morning Press* (Santa Barbara), July 19, 1925.
Mr. and Mrs. DeWitt Parshall greeted George and Carrie Steedman at a party at Edgecliffe.

———. "The Daily Round of Society." *Morning Press* (Santa Barbara), July 24, 1925.
Luncheon for Katherine at Edgecliffe.

———. "The Daily Round of Society." *Morning Press* (Santa Barbara), August 12, 1925.
Mrs. James T. Drummond of St. Louis is guest of Steedmans.

———. "The Daily Round of Society." *Morning Press* (Santa Barbara), August 12, 1925.
Katherine will leave August 19 for Michigan and then return to St. Louis.

———. "Daily Round of Society." *Morning Press* (Santa Barbara), August 20, 1925.
Katherine is en route to Michigan.

"Paintings by Byne Are Exhibited Here." *St. Louis Daily Globe-Democrat*, November 18, 1925.

1926

BOOKS

American Country Houses of Today. 1927. With a Preface by Alfred Hopkins. New York: Architectural Book Publishing Company, Inc., Paul Wenzel and Maurice Krakow, 1926, 122–24.

PERIODICALS

Bulletin of The Garden Club of America no. 9 (third series) (May 1926): 2–3, 7, 12–13.

"Special Train Brings Garden Club Hosts." *Morning Press* (Santa Barbara), April 13, 1926.
About one-third of the local members are engaged in committee work…including…. They will be assisted today by staff including…Mrs. George F. Steedman….

Official Program of the Thirteenth Annual Meeting of the Garden Club of America Held at Santa Barbara, California April 13-14-15-16, 1926: Tuesday April 13th "Casa del Herrero (Mr. and Mrs. George F. Steedman).

"Nine Gardens to be Open Tuesday." *Morning Press* (Santa Barbara), May 2, 1926.

"California Homes of George Washington Smith." *Pacific Coast Architect* 29, no. 5 (May 1926): 11–13. Reprinted; see 2001.

Kocher, A. Lawrence. "The Country House. Are We Developing an American Style?" *Architectural Record* 60, no. 5 (November 1926): 471–74. Reprinted; see 2001.

1927

BOOKS

American Art Association. *Spanish Art. Collection of the Conde de las Almenas, Madrid*. New York: American Art Association, Inc., 1927, 132, 188, 249, 318, 322, 323, 346.

Sexton, R. W. *Spanish Influence on American Architecture and Decoration*. New York: Brentano's, 1927, 105, 166.

PERIODICALS

Byne, Mildred Stapley. "Gothic Painted Ceilings from Teruel." *Art Bulletin* 9, no. 4 (1927): 341–51.

"Residence of Mr. Geo. F. Steedman, Santa Barbara, Calif. George Washington Smith, Architect." *Pacific Coast Architect* 31, no. 2 (February 1927): 76.
Photograph by J. W. Collinge. No text.

"Tea Given at School by Friends of Art." *Morning Press* (Santa Barbara), May 18, 1927.
Mrs. George Steedman is member of Society of Friends of the School of Arts.

1928

BOOKS

"George Fox Steedman." In *Harvard College Class of 1892, Report XI, 1892–1928*. Norwood, Massachusetts: Privately Printed for the Class by the Plimpton Press, 193–94.

PERIODICALS

"Society Page." *Morning Press* (Santa Barbara), April 10, 1928.
Lindbergh dinner.

Levy, Juana Neal. "Society, Affairs of the Week." *Los Angeles Times*, April 15, 1928.
Lindberg dinner.

"Women Polo Teams to Clash." *Los Angeles Times*, April 19, 1928.
Medora Steedman

"Miss K. Steedman Engaged to Marry." *New York Times*, May 17, 1928.

"Society News." *St. Louis Daily Globe-Democrat*, June 14, 1928.
Steedman/Hinckley wedding.

"Steedman-Hinckley Wedding Late Today." *St. Louis Post Dispatch*, June 14, 1928.

"Social Items." *St. Louis Post-Dispatch*, June 14, 1928.
Steedman/Hinckley wedding.

"Society News." *St. Louis Star*, June 14, 1928.
Steedman/Hinckley wedding.

"Society News." *St. Louis Daily Globe-Democrat*, June 15, 1928.
Steedman/Hinckley wedding.

"Society News." *St. Louis Star*, June 15, 1928.
Steedman/Hinckley wedding.

"Steedman-Hinckley." *New York Times*, June 16, 1928.

"Hinckley-Steedman." *New York Times*, June 17, 1928.

1929

BOOKS

Staats, H. Philip. "Gardener's Cottage, Estate of Geo. F. Steedman." In *Californian Architecture in Santa Barbara*. New York: Architectural Book Publishing Co., Inc., 1929, 117. New edition; see 1990.

PERIODICALS

"Carolyn Swartz and Partner Win Title." *Los Angeles Times*, July 14, 1929.
Medora Steedman, Kansas Open Tennis Tournament, Independence.

1930

BOOKS

Chase, Pearl, ed. *Cacti and Other Succulents*. Santa Barbara: Garden Tours Committee of the Plans and Planting Branch, Community Arts Association, 1930, facing 49.
Includes photograph of Casa del Herrero cactus garden.

PERIODICALS

"Society News." *St. Louis Daily Globe-Democrat*, October 7, 1930.
Steedman/Bass wedding.

"Medora Steedman to Wed George E. Bass." *St. Louis Post-Dispatch*, October 7, 1930.

No title. *St. Louis Daily Globe-Democrat*, November 2, 1930.
Steedman/Bass wedding.

"Social Activities." *St. Louis Post-Dispatch*, November 4, 1930.
Steedman/Bass wedding.

"Society News." *St. Louis Daily Globe-Democrat*, November 5, 1930.
Steedman/Bass wedding.

1931

PERIODICALS

"First of Five Garden Tours Will Be Sponsored Tomorrow." *Morning Press* (Santa Barbara), March 19, 1931.

"New Life for Horse Show Sure." *Los Angeles Times*, June 19, 1931.
"The following individuals who contributed money to make the show possible will serve as directors:…George F. Steedman…."

"Horse Show 'Second Nighters'… " *Morning Press* (Santa Barbara), July 25, 1931.
"Pink Boy exhibited by Mrs. George F. Steedman and ridden by John Van Dusen, third…."

"Horses Thrill Large Throng." *Los Angeles Times*, July 26, 1931.
"Polo Ponies Shown … Pink Boy exhibited by Mrs. George F. Steedman and ridden by John Van Dusen, third…."

1932

BOOKS

"George Fox Steedman." In *Harvard College Class of 1892, Report XII, 1892–1932*. Norwood, Massachusetts: Privately Printed for the Class by the Plimpton Press, 198.

1934

PERIODICALS

"Fleischmann Heads Museum." *Daily News* (Santa Barbara), January 17, 1934.
Mrs. George Fox Steedman elected to Santa Barbara Museum of Natural History Board of Trustees.

"Fleischmann Heads Museum Directorate."

Morning Press (Santa Barbara), January 17, 1934.

"Mrs. George Fox Steedman … elected to the board of new trustees."

"Garden Club Flower Show at Museum of Natural History Attracts Many Visitors." *Daily News* (Santa Barbara), March 16, 1934.

"Mrs. George R. [*sic*] Steedman was awarded the largest number of prizes, winning four firsts, three seconds, one third and an honorable mention."

"Mrs. George Steedman Takes Top Honors in Annual Flower Exhibit." *Morning Press* (Santa Barbara), March 16, 1934.

"Mrs. George F. Steedman carried off the largest number of prizes, winning four firsts, three seconds, one third and an honorable mention."

"Garden Club Will Assist Federation." *Daily News* (Santa Barbara), September 12, 1934.

"Among the Garden Club members who grew plants and showed specimens were…Mrs. George F. Steedman.…"

"The Free Lance." *NP* (Santa Barbara), October 21, 1934.

"Long hours were spent by our Garden club leaders … Mrs. George Steedman…" Pearl Chase, Ralph Stevens.

1935

PERIODICALS

"Museum Board Is Increased." *Daily News* (Santa Barbara), January 16, 1935.

"… the following trustees whose terms expire this year were reelected: Mrs. George Fox Steedman.…"

"Museum Elects Officials, Trustees Increased to 20." *Morning Press* (Santa Barbara), January 16, 1935.

"The following trustees whose terms expired this year were reelected: Mrs. George Fox Steedman.…"

"Many Sponsor Lecture on Gardens." *Morning Press* (Santa Barbara), March 6, 1935.

"… approaching lecture by Mrs. Ellen Shipman, noted landscape architect, who will speak on Italian gardens at the Montecito Country club next Monday evening.…Those who have helped…finance Mrs. Shipman's lecture are: Mrs. George Fox Steedman.…"

"Wild Life Poster Wins Medal." *Los Angeles Times*, March 6, 1935.

Presented by Mrs. George F. Steedman, chairman of the conservation committee of the Garden Club of Santa Barbara and Montecito.

"Museum Members to Inspect New Buildings at Tea Today." *Morning Press* (Santa Barbara), March 15, 1935.

"The directors are … Mrs. George Fox Steedman.…"

"Members Inspect Bird Hall in New $35,000 Wing of Museum Of Natural History Buildings." *Morning Press* (Santa Barbara), March 16, 1935.

"Mrs. George Fox Steedman [presided] at the punch table."

"Visitors from 33 States on Garden Tour." *Daily News* (Santa Barbara), April 15, 1935.

"The committee in charge of arrangements for the National Council of State Garden Clubs is…Mrs. George F. Steedman, Mrs. William R. Hart and Miss Pearl Chase."

1936

PERIODICALS

"Museum Holds Annual Meet." *Morning Press* (Santa Barbara), February 11, 1936.

Mrs. George F. Steedman is trustee of Botanic Gardens.

"G. F. Steedmans View Races." *Morning Press* (Santa Barbara), February 24, 1936.

"Gardens at Loveliest after Rain." *Morning Press* (Santa Barbara), April 10, 1936.

Garden tour.

"Garden Tours to be Held Today." *Morning Press* (Santa Barbara), July 10, 1936.

"Garden Tours Slated Today." *Morning Press* (Santa Barbara), August 7, 1936.

"The Garden of Mr. and Mrs. George Steedman, 'Casa del Herrero,' is most interesting. The house is of Spanish type and there are bird houses and an attractive grille, harmonized in effective design with the house and garden."

"Fiesta City Joy Reigns." *Los Angeles Times*, August 8, 1936.

"Casa del Herrero … were some of the famous estates thrown open to the caravan."

1937

BOOKS

"George Fox Steedman." In *Harvard College Class of 1892, Report, XIV, 1892–1937*. Norwood, Massachusetts: Privately Printed for the Class by the Plimpton Press, 63.

The copy at the Casa is annotated in Steedman's hand: "Error–This notice pertains to W. N. Duane–See Addenda to XIV Report"

"Addendum." In *Harvard College Class of 1892, Supplement to Report Number XIV, Forty-fifth Anniversary Celebration, June 22–24, 1937*. Norwood, Massachusetts: Privately Printed for the Class by the Plimpton Press, 1937, 38.

PERIODICALS

"Noted Places on Friday's Garden Tour." *Morning Press* (Santa Barbara), April 16, 1937.

"Visitors and Students See Noted Gardens." *Los Angeles Times*, August 15, 1937.

"… Casa del Herrero, where Mr. and Mrs. George F. Steedman abide on Valley Road, offered its floral beauties."

"Santa Barbara Ends Summer Garden Tours." *Los Angeles Times*, September 10, 1937.

"On Valley Road, 'Casa del Herrero,' the home of George F. Steedman, was visited. In the gardens use of Spanish decorative tile, fountains, pools and trees suggested old Spain."

"Santa Barbarans Plan Afternoons of Bridge." *Los Angeles Times*, October 17, 1937.

"Among those who remained for practice rounds were Mmes.… George F. Steedman.…"

1938

PERIODICALS

"Britons Hold Reunion." *Los Angeles Times*, March 2, 1938.

"… friends of Mrs. George Steedman of Santa Barbara.…"

1939

PERIODICALS

"Miss Du Pont Goes East." *Los Angeles Times*, April 13, 1939.

1940

PERIODICALS

"Explosion Injuries Fatal to Gordon Kenneth Grant, Noted Artist." *Santa Barbara News-Press* March 2, 1940.

"Cannon Kills Young Artist." *Los Angeles Times*, March 3, 1940.

"Gordon K. Grant Killed." *New York Times*, March 3, 1940.

"Inquest Dropped in Grant Death." *Santa Barbara News-Press*, March 3, 1940.

"Funeral Services Are Held for Gordon Kenneth Grant." *Santa Barbara News-Press*, March 4, 1940.

"Death by Cannon Termed Accident." *Los Angeles Times*, March 4, 1940.

"Poetess Is Guest." *Los Angeles Times*, March 24, 1940.

"Lunching at the Coral Casino as the guest of Mrs. George Steedman was Alice Marble, the chic tennis star, and her friend Eleanor Tennant."

"Geo. F. Steedman, Former St. Louis Man, Dies in West." *St. Louis Star-Times*, April 30, 1940.

"Geo. F. Steedman Dies in West." *St. Louis Daily Globe-Democrat*, April 30, 1940.

"George F. Steedman Will Be Buried in St. Louis." *St. Louis Star-Times*, April 30, 1940.

"George F. Steedman Funeral Tomorrow." News clipping, source unknown, April 30, 1940.

"Obituaries." *The Harvard Engineering Society Bulletin* 21, no. 1 (June 1940): 8.

1941

BOOKS

"Tours." In *Santa Barbara: A Guide to the Channel City and Its Environs*, compiled and written by the Southern California Writers' Project of the Work Project Administration. New York: Hastings House Publishers, 1941, 131, 141.

PERIODICALS

"Flower Show Winners Named." *Los Angeles Times*, April 5, 1941.

"Other winners in the large display class were Mrs. George F. Steedman.…"

1942

BOOKS

W. B. S. "George Fox Steedman." *Harvard College Class of 1892, Report XV, Fiftieth Anniversary 1942*. Norwood, Massachusetts: Privately Printed for the Class by the Plimpton Press, 1942, 401–03.

1948

PERIODICALS

"Women Busy Planning City's Concert Season." *Los Angeles Times*, December 12, 1948.

"Others who will attend the concerts are Mmes … George F. Steedman.…"

1958

PERIODICALS

"Annual Fete Set by Music Academy." *Los Angeles Times*, May 18, 1958.

"Guests have been invited also by Mmes …George Steedman.…"

1975

BOOKS

McCall, Wayne, Herb Andree, Noel Young, and Patricia Halloran. "Steedman House, 'Casa del Herrero.'" In *Santa Barbara Architecture*. Santa Barbara, California: Capra Press, 1975, 102–03.

See also: 90, 93.

1980

PERIODICALS

"Spring Benefit Time for VIMS." *Los Angeles Times*, March 20, 1980.

"Then they travel on to Montecito for a walk through the Andalusian villa, 'Casa del Herrero,' the estate of Mr. and Mrs. George Bass."

1984

BOOKS

Verey, Rosemary, and Ellen Samuels. "The Garden of Medora Bass." In *The American Woman's Garden.* Boston: Little, Brown & Company, 1984, 23–27.

PERIODICALS

Griscom, Elane. "Joe Acquistapace: An Intimate View of a Montecito Garden." *Montecito Magazine* 4, no. 1 (Spring 1984): 16–18, 50–53.

1986

PERIODICALS

Gebhard, David. "Casa del Herrero, the George F. Steedman house, Montecito, California." *Antiques* 130, no. 2 (August 1986): 280-285.

Streatfield, David. "The Gardens at Casa del Herrero." *Antiques* 130, no. 2 (August 1986): 286–293.

1987

PERIODICALS

Bree, Carmen. "Casa del Herrero (House of the Blacksmith)." *Santa Barbara* XIII, no. 3 (May/June 1987): 40–41.

1989

PERIODICALS

Baumgartner, Sydney. "West of Eden." *Horticulture* LXVII, no. 2 (February 1989): cover, 38–43.

1990

BOOKS

Staats, H. Philip. "Gardener's Cottage, Estate of Geo. F. Steedman." In *Californian Architecture in Santa Barbara.* Stamford, Conn.: Architectural Book Publishing Co., Inc., 1990, 117.

1991

BOOKS

Griswold, Mac, and Eleanor Weller. "Three Large Mediterranean Gardens." In *The Golden Age of American Gardens.* New York: Harry N. Abrams, Inc., 1991, 329–31. Includes Casa del Herrero.

Hamilton, Esley. "The Great Gifts: Steedman and Givens." In *The Way We Came. A Century of the AIA in St. Louis.* Edited by George McCue. St. Louis: Patrice Press, 1991, 49–51.

1993

BOOKS

Vogt, Elizabeth E. "Casa del Herrero." In *Montecito: California's Garden Paradise.* Santa Barbara: MIP Publishing, 1993, 124–29.

1994

BOOKS

Streatfield, David C. "Casa del Herrero." In *California Gardens: Creating a New Eden.* New York, London, and Paris: Abbeville Press Publishers, 1994, 113–18.

PERIODICALS

Colonial Homes 20 (February 1994): 70–75. Churchill, Maria, "Casa del Herrero." *Montecito Magazine* 14, no.2 (Fall 1994): cover, 14–18, 20–21, 86–87.

1995

PERIODICALS

Goodrich, Jean Smith. "Casa del Herrero." *Noticias* 41, no. 2 (Summer 1995): 21–43.

1996

PERIODICALS

Goodrich, Jean Smith. "Tile at the Casa del Herrero." *Noticias* 42, no. 3 (Autumn 1996): 59–62.

Trenta, Ursula R. "Estudio sobre un artesonado turolense existente en Italia." *Separata de Teruel* no. 35 (1996).

1998

BOOKS

Myrick, David F. "George F. Steedman and Casa del Herrero." In *Montecito and Santa Barbara. From Farms to Estates.* Volume I. Pasadena, California: Pentrex Media Group, 1998, 206–07; 213–14.

1999

BOOKS

Tinniswood, Adrian. "Casa del Herrero." In *The Arts & Crafts House.* New York: Watson-Guptill Publications, 1999, 92–95.

PERIODICALS

Smith, Michael. "A Love Affair with Spain." *Santa Barbara* 25, no. 3 (Summer 1999): cover, 58–63.

2000

PERIODICALS

Massey, James C., and Shirley Maxwell. "Spanish Colonial Revival." *Old House Journal* 28, no. 6 (December 2000): cover, 6, 59, 64.

2001

BOOKS

"George F. Steedman Residence, 1922–1925." In *George Washington Smith: An Architect's Scrapbook,* edited and with an Introduction by Marc Appleton. Los Angeles: Tailwater Press, 2001: 106–09. Reprinted from *Pacific Coast Architect* (May 1926) and *Architectural Record* (November 1926)

Masson, Kathryn. "Casa del Herrero." In *Santa Barbara Style,* with principal photography by James Chen. New York: Rizzoli, 2001, 66–75.

2002

BOOKS

Lewis, Lucinda, photography, and Jan Smithen, text. *Sun-Drenched Gardens: The Mediterranean Style.* New York: Harry N. Abrams, Inc., 2002, 63–64, 84, 88–89, 120, 139, 144, 163.

2003

BOOKS

Gabarda, Felix Brun. *Artesonados mudéjares de Teruel en el extranjero.* Teruel, Spain: Publisher, 2003.

2004

PERIODICALS

Mitchell, Collin. "A Holiday House." *California Homes* (November/December 2004): 100–07.

2005

BOOKS

Gebhard, Patricia. "The Steedman House." In *George Washington Smith. Architect of the Spanish Colonial Revival.* Salt Lake City: Gibbs Smith, Publisher, 2005, front, 76–81.

2006

PERIODICALS

Crowell, Judy. "Casa del Herrero." *St. Louis Seasons* (Fall 2006): cover, 64–67.

2007

BOOKS

Appleton, Marc. "Casa del Herrero." In *California Mediterranean.* New York: Rizzoli, 2007, 36–45. A plan appears on page 15.

Keaton, Diane, and D. J. Waldie. "Casa del Herrero." In *California Romantica.* New York: Rizzoli, 2007, 188–205.

2008

PERIODICALS

Irwin, Sue. "Cottage Life at Casa del Herrero." *Montecito Magazine* 28, no. 2 (Fall 2008): cover, 20–26, 28, 30.

2009

PERIODICALS

Rolens, Sam. "In the Home of the Centaur." *Santa Barbara Independent,* March 22, 2009. National Historic Landmark.

Wilson, D. Lorraine. "On the Town." *News Press* (Santa Barbara) April 26, 2009. Includes "National Historic Landmark," with photograph.

ARCHIVAL MATERIAL

George Steedman Archives, Casa del Herrero, Santa Barbara.

George Washington Smith Collection, Architecture and Design Collection, University Art Museum, University of California, Santa Barbara.

Julia Morgan Papers, Special Collections, University Archives, California Polytechnic State University, San Luis Obispo.

Lockwood de Forest III Collection, Environmental Design Archives, University of California, Berkeley.

Lutah Maria Riggs Collection, Architecture and Design Collection, University Art Museum, University of California, Santa Barbara.

UNPUBLISHED MATERIAL

Griscom, Elaine. Santa Barbara Regional Oral History Clearinghouse. Santa Barbara Historical Museum. *Joe Acquistapace.* January 14, 1984.

Kastner, Virginia. "Arthur Byne, Mildred Stapley Byne, and the Spanish Colonial Revival." Master's thesis, University of California, Santa Barbara, 1989.

Rodríguez Thiessen, Victoria. *Byne and Stapley: Scholars, Dealers, and Collectors of Spanish Decorative Arts,* Master's thesis, Program in the History of the Decorative Arts, Cooper-Hewitt, National Design Museum and Parsons School of Design, 1998.